THE LAST METHOD

BOOK ONE

THE HERO'S JOURNEY

ANDREW COLTON

WATCHTOWER

Published in the United States by Watchtower Press (New York), an imprint of Neumeyer, Inc.

Email: info@thelastmethod.com

Library of Congress Control Number: 2025924802

ISBN 979-8-9937247-0-6 (Paperback edition)

ISBN 979-8-9937247-1-3 (Ebook edition)

History is the ultimate weapon, because it harnesses time itself. Used correctly, the past can alter the present. What other invention can do that?

— GAAL DORNICK

CONTENTS

INTRODUCTION

The Cycle of Repackaged Hope

The self-help industry is expected to reach a staggering $14 billion market value by 2025. It's everywhere — flooding bookstores, filling conference halls, dominating podcasts, and turning everyday influencers into personal development gurus. While it has undoubtedly transformed the lives of millions, it also carries a long shadow of skepticism. To some, it remains little more than snake oil for the soul — a landscape filled with lofty promises, questionable credentials, and advice that often lacks real substance. Many try it. Some benefit. But a great number are left feeling disillusioned.

Unlike clinical psychology, which — despite its own limitations — is grounded in empirical research and ethical oversight, self-help relies more heavily on market demand than on peer review. It is largely unregulated, with effectiveness often determined by popularity rather than rigor.

Readers are left to navigate the sea of advice on their own, deciding what resonates, what works, and what's worth discarding.

At the core of the industry lies a quiet paradox: in order to thrive, it must keep you feeling perpetually dissatisfied. Self-help positions itself as the gateway to happiness, success, and transformation — yet its business model depends on you feeling that you're not quite enough. You're always one book, one seminar, or one coaching session away from the life you truly want. The result is a cycle of consumption in which growth is promised but rarely sustained.

To be clear, the tools offered by the self-help world can be valuable. But the industry is also driven by manufactured urgency. Its success depends not just on inspiration, but on keeping you wanting more. Tried-and-true concepts are rebranded, renamed, and repackaged as proprietary systems. Personal growth becomes a product, and the more insecure you feel, the more likely you are to buy again.

Over time, these returns diminish. The hope that brought you to self-help in the first place begins to wear thin. And while the market keeps expanding, the individual may find themselves in a loop — collecting wisdom but never quite breaking through.

The Illusion of Novelty

At the heart of the industry's fundamental problem is its tendency to present timeless wisdom as if it were newly discovered. Many self-help books and programs are built on ideas that have existed for decades — in some cases, centuries. Concepts like mindfulness, visualization, and goal-setting have long histories in both ancient philosophy and modern psychology. Yet in the hands of marketers and influencers, they are often rebranded as exclusive systems, sold with fresh terminology and packaged as groundbreaking.

Take, for example, the modern productivity guru who introduces a "revolutionary" method for time management — only to reveal, upon closer inspection, another variation of prioritizing urgent versus important tasks, a concept that has existed in business and psychology for decades — often a simplified version of Eisenhower's Urgent/Important Matrix from the 1950s.

Or consider the influencer who markets a "breakthrough" morning routine system, when similar practices have been recommended by everyone from Benjamin Franklin to military strategists throughout history. Similarly, principles like positive thinking, now ubiquitous in pop psychology, trace back to the 19th-century New Thought movement. What is old becomes new again — not by evolution, but by rebranding.

Life coaching offers another example. Many coaching programs repurpose basic mentorship or cognitive-behavioral strategies but present them under proprietary labels. While some coaches provide meaningful guidance, others dilute and repackage foundational psychological methods without context or depth, reducing complex ideas into oversimplified formulas.

The result is fragmentation — a growing list of competing ideologies, each claiming to be the definitive path to personal success. In this crowded marketplace, clarity gives way to confusion. And instead of fostering genuine transformation, the constant rotation of "new" systems often creates doubt, fatigue, or even paralysis. The search for a better life becomes cluttered with noise — each book or seminar insisting that its framework is the one that finally holds the key.

The Commercialization of Insecurity

The self-help industry thrives on a manufactured sense of urgency — and on the subtle suggestion that you are not yet whole. Its success depends on convincing people they are incomplete, and that the answers lie outside themselves. In doing so, it creates a powerful cycle: after finishing one book or program, the message is clear — there's still more work to do. Another book. Another course. Another method. You're never quite finished.

Ironically, many of these teachings emphasize self-reliance, inner peace, and personal power — yet the industry that promotes them often profits by cultivating dependence. It sells the idea that transformation is just out of reach, and that with the right investment, the next breakthrough will finally come. This contradiction undermines the very values it claims to uphold.

Worse, the industry often simplifies complex life challenges into generic advice and one-size-fits-all frameworks. Mental health struggles, career dissatisfaction, or relationship issues are rarely resolved by slogans or simplified checklists. And yet, that is how many self-help products are marketed — promising quick solutions to problems that are deeply personal and nuanced.

When the promised transformation fails to materialize, the result isn't just disappointment — it's self-blame. Instead of questioning the system, individuals question themselves. *Did I not try hard enough? Did I misunderstand the process? Maybe this just doesn't work for me.* The very people seeking growth and clarity end up feeling more uncertain than when they began.

That said, we should acknowledge that the self-help world is not without merit. For many, it has been a source of motivation, inspiration, and useful tools. Some books truly do offer practical guidance, especially when they connect with a reader's specific needs and values. The problem arises not from the presence of insight, but from the packaging — when ideas are stripped of context, inflated with promises, and sold with more concern for profit than for genuine impact.

A Different Approach: Empowerment Through Transparency

In the midst of recycled ideas and commercial exploitation, there is room for a different kind of approach — one grounded in clarity, transparency, and respect for the reader's intelligence. *The Last Method* represents this shift.

Rather than claiming to hold a proprietary secret to success, this book series offers something simpler and more honest: a curated framework that draws from established psychological principles, philosophical traditions, and behavioral science. It doesn't pretend to reinvent the wheel. It doesn't trade in mysticism or hype. Instead, it lays out the tools that have stood the test of time — not as rigid systems to adopt, but as resources to explore. Even the way this book is structured reflects this philosophy: it invites you to slow down, to pause between ideas, and to engage more thoughtfully with each concept — creating space for reflection rather than rushing toward answers.

This method avoids the trap of mystifying personal growth. It acknowledges that the most meaningful change is not about uncovering some hidden truth — it's about finally understanding the tools that have always been available, and using them with intention.

By presenting self-improvement as a toolkit rather than a branded ideology, The Last Method gives the power back to the reader. You are not asked to follow a guru, nor to subscribe to a specific doctrine. You are invited to experiment, to select what resonates, and to shape your own path.

Personal growth is not a fixed sequence. It's not something that can be mass-produced or universally prescribed. That's why this approach emphasizes flexibility, personal agency, and lifelong integration — not a single turning point, but an ongoing process of alignment.

In a landscape crowded with promises, The Last Method makes a different one: not to deliver transformation for you, but to equip you with what you need to pursue it on your own terms.

The Ethics of Personal Development: Balancing Commercialism with Authenticity

As the self-help industry continues to grow, so too does the responsibility of those who contribute to it. The rapid commercialization of personal development has raised ethical concerns — particularly in a landscape dominated by aggressive marketing strategies, inflated promises, and influencer-driven content. Too often, the pursuit of profit eclipses the commitment to genuine impact.

Creators in this space have a choice: to serve their audience or to exploit them. The best books, programs, and teachings don't just inspire — they respect the complexity of personal growth. They avoid oversimplifying life's challenges and resist the temptation to reduce transformation to a list of quick fixes. These works don't promise perfection. Instead, they offer grounded guidance, presented with humility and integrity.

The demand for greater transparency is not just a passing trend — it's an essential correction. In an era where personal development is increasingly commodified, it's critical that those who publish ideas, lead programs, or build platforms operate with clear ethical intentions. Influence should come with accountability.

But the responsibility doesn't lie solely with creators. Readers, too, must learn to engage critically. It's tempting to chase the next solution, the next insight, the next source of motivation — especially when life feels uncertain. But transformation is not something that can be consumed. It has to be lived. The path is rarely linear. It's often messy, uncomfortable, and slow.

The Last Method doesn't claim to be a blueprint for success. This book series isn't designed to offer universal answers. What it offers is a framework — a structure that invites exploration, experimentation, and self-responsibility. It encourages readers to customize their own approach, and to view personal development not as a product to acquire, but as a journey to engage with — honestly, imperfectly, and fully.

Looking Ahead: A Future Built on Self-Empowerment

The future of personal development doesn't lie in bigger promises or flashier systems. It lies in self-awareness, critical thinking, and the ability to act with intention. The next evolution of the self-help industry must move beyond quick fixes and recycled advice toward practices that foster genuine, sustainable change.

The Last Method exists as a response to that shift. It is not a branded formula, nor a promise of overnight transformation. It's a guide — a curated map of tested tools and ideas — designed to put you, the reader, in charge of your own growth.

This book series does not ask you to believe in magic. It does not ask you to surrender your discernment. Instead, it challenges you to engage deeply, to examine your own patterns, and to reclaim authorship of your story.

Because real transformation isn't something you buy — it's something you build.

The tools for change have always been within reach. What's often missing is the structure, the clarity, and the courage to use them with consistency. This book series offers that structure — not as a prescription, but as a starting point. What you do with it will always be up to you.

Personal development should not be a marketplace of dependency. It should be a shared human experience — a space where we learn, stumble, and grow without pretending that there's a single answer for everyone.

That is the future this approach points toward. And that is the work we begin now.

A Note on Style

You may notice something different
about the rhythm of this book.
The lines are shorter.
The thoughts are more spacious.
The pacing is intentional.

This isn't a design trick.
It's a decision — made to help you slow down.
To hear your own thoughts
in the quiet between mine.
To breathe between ideas.
To feel the weight of a sentence before rushing past it.

In a world that moves too fast,
we've learned to skim everything —
including ourselves.

This format invites you to pause.
To reflect.
To engage not just intellectually, but personally.

The white space isn't filler.
It's room —
for you.

The Power of Reflection: Journaling as a Tool for Growth

Science now echoes what sages have long intuited:
writing reshapes the mind.

When you set pen to paper — or fingers to keys —
you ignite a chorus of brain regions:
language, emotion, movement, memory.
Unlike fleeting thoughts or spoken words,
writing slows the current,
carving space for hidden truths to surface.

This is why reflection becomes more than a pause —
it's a gateway.
A way to distill the rush of experience
into moments of meaning.

It takes the tangle of feeling
and weaves it into clarity,
giving form to what lingers in the mind's shadows.

Journaling — simple yet profound —
becomes a vital instrument in your transformation.

What starts as words on a page
grows into something greater:
a lens, revealing the currents beneath your choices;
a compass, guiding your evolving path;
a quiet ally, bearing witness to your growth.

This act forges new pathways in the brain,
linking awareness to action.
It sharpens vague stirrings into defined insights,
building resilience in both mind and heart.
You're not merely noting events.
You're uncovering their meaning.
You begin to spot the stories you've carried —
and realize you hold the power to recast them.

The *Last Method* isn't meant to be read passively —
it's meant to be lived.
Your journal is the space where this begins,
capturing fleeting insights before they fade,
uncovering patterns,
sharpening intentions.

This isn't mere intellectual exercise —
it's a call to embody your truth.
Journaling makes that embodiment tangible.

The Sacred Space of Your Story

As you navigate these pages,
moments will stir —
a truth will resonate,
a question will linger,
a memory will surface.

Don't let them slip away.
Your journal is where they take root,
where you probe their weight,
where you glean their lessons.

It's more than a record of insights —
it's a sacred vessel for your story:
the adventures you embraced or evaded,
the fears that shaped your steps,
the voices — near or distant —
that molded your vision.
Each entry becomes a marker,
leading you back to your core.

Journaling reveals rhythms you hadn't seen —
the cycles you repeat,
the words you choose to frame your days,
the narratives that either confine or free you.

It's not mere recollection.
It's creation, an act of active authorship.
Each entry, each honest glimpse,
becomes a cornerstone of a truer self.

You're not just inscribing thoughts.
You're crafting a new way of being —
step by step toward the person you're becoming.

Your Path to Powerful Practice

There's no single right way to journal —
only one wrong way:
not beginning at all.

The beauty of journaling lies in its freedom.
Cast aside rules.
Forget grammar.
Abandon the urge to sound profound or complete.
Let it be messy and raw.
Let it tangle and contradict.
Let it feel like a draft —
for you are always becoming.

Start with questions —
our minds are built to chase them,
unraveling answers over time,
sometimes long after the pen rests.
These questions are portals,
and your words, the keys.

Begin with what stirs:
What sparked joy in my day?
How have I grown in the past year,
and where am I still stretching?
What old habits am I ready to shed?

Then venture deeper:
What trials have I faced,
and what wisdom have they offered?
What fear holds me now, and what does it reveal?

When you're ready, pierce through the noise:
What conviction, if released, would shift my world?
Where am I hiding from my own truth?
What part of me is stirring to break free?

These aren't mere prompts —
they're invitations to meet yourself.
Answer with honesty,
and your inner voice will emerge —
not in grand proclamations,
but in quiet truths you didn't know you held.

You write for no one else.
You write to rouse yourself.
Your journal craves not elegance,
but truth —
unfiltered, unrefined, alive.

Let the ink splatter.
Let the sentences trail off.
Let clarity stumble in late.
The revelations lie not in perfection —
but in the raw pulse of what's real.

Making This Your Practice

Whether you choose pen or screen matters little.
Some find clarity in the slow dance of ink on paper.
Others prefer the swift capture of digital notes,
always at hand to revisit.
The form is secondary —
the truth is what counts.

As you move through this book and those to come,
keep your journal close.
Make it part of your practice —
a constant companion in your becoming.

When a phrase strikes a chord:
Pause.
Growth takes root in the stillness.
Capture the raw, unfiltered thought —
no need for polished words.

Ask:
How does this reflect my life now?
Capture it before it dissolves into the day's hum.

Consider one small step before turning the page —
a shift in how you see,
a boundary you'll uphold,
a truth you'll face unflinching.

This is how reading transcends mere consumption.
It becomes a dialogue —
a bridge between the words on the page
and the self you're shaping.
With time, the clearest voice in the room
will not be the author's.
It will be yours.

The Edge of Transformation

Journaling isn't about cataloging your days.
It's about claiming them.
A dialogue with your deepest self —
guiding you toward clarity,
insight,
and a life that unfolds with purpose.

Your journal is more than a ledger of days —
it's where you begin to shape them.
Each line you write sparks a quiet shift,
a step from who you've been
toward who you're called to be.

The blank page is not barren —
it hums with potential,
awaiting your courage to give it voice.
It seeks only your truth,
not perfection,
not performance —
just presence.

This is the edge of transformation.
A mirror to your essence.
A summons to rediscover yourself —
beyond the clamor,
beyond the masks,
beyond the doubts.

One question remains:
Will you step forward
and meet yourself on the page?

❧

1

LIVE YOUR LIFE BEFORE LIFE LEAVES YOU

Life is fleeting —
not a poetic flourish,
but the starkest truth we face.
And yet, strangely,
it's the one truth we try hardest to avoid.

We weave elaborate distractions —
endless tasks,
quests for status,
cravings for ease —
to blur the reality
that each moment spent
is a moment gone forever.

Death, impartial and quiet,
levels all.

No wealth, no fame,
no title spares you.
Magnate or laborer,
icon or unknown —
your hours will end.
The world will turn.
Dawn will break.
And those who leaned on you
will find their way forward.

Picture your own funeral for a moment —
not to be morbid,
but to wake up.

Mourners gather, eyes wet with loss.
Words of love are spoken.

But soon — startlingly soon —
life resumes.
Messages pile up.
Obligations persist.

Your name, once vivid,
softens into echoes,
then stillness.
The job you vacated is refilled.
The life you once curated with such precision
is packed away into memories,
then into silence.

Sit with that for a moment.
Linger here,
not to despair,
but to unshackle.
Embracing this truth
dissolves the chains.

You see how much of life has been a performance —
for unseen judges,
for fleeting praise,
for a script you didn't write.

We live as if we're building statues to ourselves —
empires of achievement,
hoards of possessions,
polished facades.

We aim to leave a legacy,
as if permanence were possible.
But the truth is,
legacy is mostly a myth.

The monuments we construct —
whether literal or symbolic —
do not hold back the tide of time.

Pyramids touch the sky,
yet their builders' names are dust.

Empires once spanned horizons;
now their stones frame selfies.
Caesar lingers in memory —
but who recalls the countless souls
who paved his roads,
who dreamed their own fleeting dreams?

Everything you build with such care —
the empire, the reputation,
the carefully crafted life —
dissolves like morning mist.
Gone. Given away. Forgotten.

Your name will fade completely
within two generations, maybe three.
Think about that for a moment.
Can you name your great-grandparents?
Do you know their full names, their struggles,
what kept them awake at night,
what made their hearts race with hope?
Probably not.

This should clarify something:
ninety-nine percent of your daily worries
are utterly, magnificently pointless —
noise mistaken for substance.

We live on a rock spinning a thousand miles per hour
through a universe containing four hundred million
trillion trillion stars.

That's a four with twenty-three zeros
trailing behind it.
And you're going to be dead soon. Me too.

If you can hold that awareness —
even for a moment each day —
you'll find something unexpected:
peace.

The knowledge that none of this matters
in the way you thought it did
doesn't diminish your life —
it liberates you to actually live it.

This is not nihilism.
This is clarity.
This is the doorway to freedom.

To see the futility of chasing forever
frees you to live for now.

You are no longer required
to carve your name into time.
Live for what rings true —
not for history's fading gaze.

When you accept that the world will forget you,
you stop needing it to remember you.
And in that space, a different kind of life emerges —
one not built on image, but on essence.

You stop striving to impress
and start striving to feel.
You stop chasing recognition
and start chasing aliveness.

Freedom blooms —
not in defying mortality,
but in embracing its truth.

Knowing this truth changes everything.
It strips away the illusions
we've built our lives upon.

The time to live is now.

The Illusion of Permanence

We step into roles without pause —
professional,
parent,
caregiver,
achiever,
each with its own lines,
its own costume,
its own weight of expectations.

We play the part, speak the script,
move through days as if being seen rightly
proves we live rightly.

But this act is rarely for us.
It's for a faceless audience we conjure,
but cannot name.

We chase accolades not for joy,
but for their gleam in others' eyes.
We gather possessions not for need,
but to signal worth —
status,
taste,
success.

We pour ourselves into roles that sap our spirit,
clinging to titles that shine briefly
in emails or on business cards soon discarded.

Yet a quiet unease lingers —
a whisper that none of it holds
the meaning we seek.

The tragedy isn't in conforming —
it's in forgetting we do.

We act as if the world is watching —
carefully evaluating our every move,
assigning points for how stylish,
successful,
or socially accepted we appear to be.

But the truth cuts sharp:
no one watches so closely.
Others are lost in their own doubts,
their own roles, their own hurried lives.
And just too busy to track yours.

The outfit you fretted over this morning?
Forgotten before lunch.
The awkward comment
you replayed in your head for hours?
No one else noticed.
The flaw you think defines you?
It doesn't even make the footnotes
of someone else's story.

And if some people don't like you?
Over time, it will make you stronger.
It's fine.
They don't like you.
Guess what?
Half the people at every party
you've ever attended
didn't like you either.

But here's the truth:
They're not thinking much about you.
They're thinking about themselves —
their own fears,
their own inadequacies,
their own endless inner noise.

You start to realize
this is just people talking at the barber shop,
gossip as old as humanity itself.
Throughout all of history,
people have whispered,
judged,
speculated.

You can notice it if you want,
but it carries no real venom.
It's not substantial.
It's not true.
It's just words
dissolving into air.

The sooner you learn
that other people's opinions
don't have to touch you,
don't have to shape you,
don't have to matter —
the freer you become.

And yet we keep dancing.
We trade our finite days for gold stars that fade,
trophies that tarnish,
and praise that evaporates.

We live as if permanence can be earned —
as if the right combination of effort and image
will secure us a place in the memory of the world.

But permanence is an illusion.
Even the grandest legacies
crumble under time's patient tide.

We have been gaslit by a culture
that sells significance as a product.
It tells us we are only as valuable as we are visible —
that worth is measured by metrics:
followers,
income,
productivity.
It insists meaning must be seen to exist.

But here's the truth:
visibility is not the same as value.
When you let others' opinions dictate your choices,
you trade your potential for their comfort —
and neither of you gains anything real.

This is why you procrastinate,
why doubt wraps itself around every decision,
why perfectionism becomes paralysis —
not protection, but prison.

This is why you wake each morning
and avoid the very work
that would move you forward,
trading progress for comfort,
potential for the familiar ache
of staying exactly where you are.

You are so afraid of judgment,
you don't take any risks at all.

You can't control what lives in someone else's mind,
so why let it govern yours?
Why grant it power over your choices,
your days, your one unrepeatable life?

Your time is too valuable for that—
too finite, too sacred
to spend defending yourself
against thoughts you'll never change.

You have important work to do,
a life that's wild and precious
and entirely your own —
waiting for you to stop asking permission
and simply begin.

Wake up to this:
You could be the most admired person in the room
and still feel empty.
You can claim every prize
and still not know yourself.

The world's cheers seduce —
but lean too close,
and they drown your own voice.

External validation is not oxygen.
It's carbon monoxide.

It doesn't nourish you —
it numbs you.
It doesn't sustain life —
it steals it slowly,
without a sound.

The moment you shed the performance
is the moment your true life takes root.

This isn't an invitation to abandon responsibility
or retreat from the world.

It's an invitation to show up differently —
more honestly,
more fully.
To make choices
that are not dictated by approval or escape,
but by alignment with your core.

To step off the stage,
cast off the guise,
and meet yourself
in the raw light of truth.

Because the most powerful standing ovation
you will ever receive

is the one you give yourself —
quietly,
resolutely —
when you live in a way that needs no audience.

When you stop building monuments to yourself,
you start building a life that is actually yours.

When Forgetting Becomes a Habit

If life's transience is so undeniable,
why do we live as if time were boundless?

Because oblivion is seductive.

We don't merely sidestep our mortality —
we lose sight of our vitality.

We cloak ourselves in habits,
in the churn of tasks,
in the hum of ceaseless doing —
not from apathy,
but from dread.

Maybe harsh words at the table
turned a holiday into wreckage,
or work swallowed you whole again —
another cancelled plan,
another apology wearing thin.

Years dissolve this way,
traded for distractions that leave no trace,
for late nights that promise meaning
but deliver only absence.

It's effortless, really —
to become so stressed about living
that you forget the point entirely:
to actually live,
to be present for the moments
that slip past while you're elsewhere,
chasing what doesn't matter.

To hold life's brevity in view
demands transformation.
And transformation unsettles.

So we weave defenses —
not with grand gestures,
but with subtle evasions.
We craft polished personas,
adept at seeming whole
while our true selves wait,
unseen, unvoiced.

Day by day,
we barter presence for motion,
truth for approval.

We grow so skilled at playing the part
that we scarcely notice
the person beneath receding.
Forgetting,
thread by thread,
becomes a pattern.
And that pattern becomes a life.

The great tragedy isn't our end —
it's that we don't truly live while we're still here.

Not for lack of capacity,
but for fear of what living demands:
the bravery to stand exposed,
the resolve to speak truth,
the fortitude to shed
what dims our essence.

To reclaim your life,
first reclaim your gaze —
see where you perform,
where you retreat,
where you've begun to fade
within the contours of your own days.

Only then can you unravel the quiet illusions,
stepping into a life that answers not to fear,
but to the call of your own becoming.

The Antidote to Regret

Regret doesn't strike like lightning.
It whispers — soft at first,
gaining weight with each passing year.
It begins in small lapses:
a hesitation, a missed chance,
a truth left unspoken.

Easy to dismiss at first —
life presses on,
the moment wasn't right,
later will suffice.

But whispers turn to echoes,
and echoes to a persistent pang,
felt in the hush of quiet hours.
Not sharp enough to wound,
but steady enough to linger.

We picture regret as grand failures —
bold risks untaken,
daring paths untraveled.

But the deepest regrets are quieter:
They are the moments we abandoned ourselves.
The words we never said.
The dreams we put off.
The boundaries we didn't hold.

The versions of ourselves we buried beneath fear,
duty,
or decorum.

Ask those nearing life's close,
and their words converge:

I wish I had expressed how I truly felt.
I wish I hadn't cared so much what others thought.
I wish I'd had the courage to live the life I wanted —
not the one others carved for me.

Rarely do people regret not working more hours
or buying more things.
They regret not living.

The tragedy isn't that life is short.
The tragedy is that we act like it isn't.

We act as if tomorrow is assured,
as if we can defer what matters most.
But time is no contract —
it's a fleeting gift,
its duration unwritten.

We spend our days chasing goals that don't satisfy us,
fulfilling obligations we didn't choose,
and clinging to versions of ourselves
we've long outgrown.

We convince ourselves it's noble to wait —
to delay joy,
to suppress desire,
to postpone truth —
because now isn't the right time.

But the stark truth is this:
now is your only certainty.
You have this moment
to cease betraying your own heart.
To stop performing
and start being.

To reach out to the one you miss.
To voice what's been caged.
To turn from what diminishes you
and toward what ignites you.
To embrace what daunts you —
not for its ease,
but for its truth.

Time to walk away from what drains you
and toward what fuels you.
Time to do the thing that scares you —
not because it's easy,
but because it's real.

This is your call to act.
No flawless blueprint required.
No external blessing needed.
No certainty demanded.

Only the courage to begin —
here,
in this breath,
in this now.

Regret grows from lingering too long
in the shadow of who you might be.
Its antidote is to choose yourself —
today, with time still in your hands.

The longer you wait for permission,
the heavier the cost of inaction becomes,
until one day you realize —
you traded possibility for safety
that never came.

This is why the time is now.
Not because tomorrow may never come,
but because today is all you truly have.

Each moment you defer your becoming
is a moment you cannot reclaim —
and the life you're meant to live
grows fainter with each delay.

The Invitation to Live Now

This book is not a mere lens —
it's a threshold.
Not just a summons to awaken —
but a map for action.
It shatters the myths that bind you:

That your value lies in what you produce.
That your dreams must wait until others are satisfied.
That joy is a reward for depletion.
That readiness will arrive in some distant tomorrow.

But tomorrow is a phantom.
And delay is a quiet theft.

This journey moves beyond insight —
it calls for courage.
It urges you to cease deferring your life
and equips you to claim it —
here, in this moment.

Stop waiting.

For certainty.
For assurance.
For the season when burdens lift or fears dissolve.
For the fabled "perfect moment" that never comes.

We call it prudence, caution, duty.
But too often, it's avoidance —
and the price is your existence.

Many live as if life were a prelude —
a practice run for a truer performance,
where we'll speak the words we meant,
love with unguarded hearts,
choose the path that calls our name.

But this is no rehearsal.
The stage is set.
The lights are on.
The moment is now.

The call to live fully —
worn thin by slogans and social scrolls —
holds a fierce, unshakable truth:
a summons to aliveness.

Recall the fire in Robin Williams' voice
in *Dead Poets Society*,
eyes alight with urgency as he declared, *Carpe diem*.
Or think of Thoreau in his cabin at Walden Pond,
yearning to *"suck out all the marrow of life."*

These aren't just literary or cinematic moments —
they're the spiritual DNA of what it means to live
with intention.
The pulse of a life lived awake.

To be alive is not to dazzle —
it's to be present.
To feel the sun's warmth and not rush past it.
To hold a conversation and actually listen.
To rise each morning with something that stirs you —
not in some far-off future,
but today.

Yet beware of the trap:
Aliveness is not the spectacle we're sold.
It's not all cliff dives and passport stamps.
It's not about amassing more.
It's about choosing what resonates —
and letting go of what doesn't.

Our world equates frenzy with meaning,
busyness with purpose.
The "full life" is peddled as a tally:
curated adventures checked off,
milestones broadcast,
triumphs imposed.

But motion without meaning,
intensity without introspection
is mere noise.

A life brimming with exploits
can still echo with emptiness
if it strays from truth.

True aliveness is often quiet.
It's the resolve to stay present when escape is easier.
The courage to say *no* when the world demands *yes*.
The stillness to hear your own heart
amid the clamor of expectations.
To live now is not to crowd your days.
It's to clear space within your soul.

There is a shadow side to *carpe diem*
that is rarely named —
a frantic chase to make every second count
can bind you as tightly as inaction.

We grow anxious about wasting time,
terrified of missing out,
enslaved by urgency.
But the fear isn't wasted time —
it's wasting who we are.

Living fully isn't a race against mortality.
It's an embrace of life.
It begins when you shift from asking,
What must I do?
to *What makes me come alive —*
and what will I release to guard that life?

For me, living now is presence —
not just occupying space,
but inhabiting my choices,
my truth, my body.

It's noticing the sunlight's dance across a quiet room.
It's staying in the conversation that matters,
even when it cuts deep.
It's choosing depth over display —
not for ease,
but for truth.

Living now is listening for what seeks to unfold —
even if it challenges the life you've built.
It's daring to grow,
to become.

Because living fully isn't about intensity —
it's about integrity.
That begins not in some distant dawn,
but here,
now.

The clock moves forward.
But your time is still yours.
What will you make of it?

The Unfinished Journey

A full life is not a place to arrive —
but a series of awakenings,
an ongoing dialogue between who you are
and who you're yet to become.

It calls you to dwell in balance —
to embrace the fire of *carpe diem*
while heeding the calm of *know thyself*.
To relish the present —
yet ponder its deeper pulse.
To chase what stirs you,
but pause to ask if it's truly yours.

Fulfillment doesn't spring from a tally of feats
or a race toward another's vision of triumph.
It blooms when your choices resonate
with the truths you hold most dear.

The question isn't
How much can I cram into my days?
but
What makes my days feel alive?

And often, the answers aren't grand.
They're subtle.
Hidden in plain sight.

The beauty of this journey lives
in the small moments.
A moment of clarity on a solitary path.
The resolve to stay present in a tense exchange.
The courage to voice your heart
when silence tempts.

These are the moments that shape us —
not the spectacular, but the sincere.
Not the loud, but the enduring.

The world will urge you toward markers of success —
tallies of worth, measures of acclaim.
But meaning lies elsewhere —
in the choice to be yourself
when conformity beckons.

In the presence you bring to those you cherish.
In the risks you take,
not for praise,
but for your truest self.

As the poet Mary Oliver asked:
"What is it you plan to do
with your one wild and precious life?"

This is no mere musing —
it's a call you'll answer again and again,
across the evolving landscape of your days.

Your answers will shift.
They should.

This journey is just beginning.
You are not complete —
you are unfolding.
Each step forward,
each choice made with care,
is a spark for the chapters yet to come.

2

MYTHOLOGY AND PERSONAL TRANSFORMATION

We often view myths as relics —
tales etched in ancient stone,
preserved in epic verse,
or echoed in the worlds of big-budget movies.

Stories of deities and beasts,
heroic quests and fated trials,
noble deeds and enchanted swords.

Compelling, perhaps,
but distant —
relegated to the realm of fantasy.

Yet myths were never meant to gather dust.
They are not mere stories —
they are guides.

Long before psychology labeled our struggles,
before self-help filled shelves
with formulas and frameworks,
myths served a vital role:
they gave form to the intangible.
They wove symbols for what defies words —
yearning, dread, purpose, pain, transcendence.

At their core,
myths are mirrors of human existence —
not of the world's surface,
but of the soul's journey through it.
This is why they endure.
For in our quest for meaning and selfhood,
we are not so far from the seekers of old.

Our castles may be cities made of concrete,
our runes replaced by screens,
our dragons now deadlines and doubts —
but the inner landscape remains untamed.

The ache for purpose.
The brush with despair.
The pull to feel chosen.
The fear of falling short.
These are not new burdens —
they are timeless.

To cast myths aside as outdated or obsolete
is to overlook the architecture of our becoming.

You're already living within myths,
perhaps unknowingly —
chasing an elusive happily-ever-after,
fleeing a fall from grace,
seeking a cure to make you whole.

Our culture spins these patterns ceaselessly —
in songs, films, ads, ideals.
We don't outgrow myths.
We simply stop seeing ourselves in them.
And in that blindness,
we lose the power to reshape them.

Transformation begins not by rejecting myth,
but by recognizing its presence —
by claiming the pen to rewrite your story.

Mythology doesn't demand belief
in gods or mystic creatures.
It calls for a bolder faith —
in the possibility that your life holds a purpose
beyond what you've been taught to suppress.

This purpose isn't bestowed.
It's crafted —
through struggle,
revelation,
and the daring to step beyond the known.

As you turn these pages,
prepare to meet the myths within you —
and begin the work of forging your own anew.

The Mythic Mind

Deep within you lies a realm logic cannot reach.
It speaks not in charts or calculations,
nor bends to what's popular or practical.

It appears in images and symbols,
stirs in dreams and lucid visions,
knows truths your reason has yet to grasp.

This is the *mythic mind* —
where meaning blooms in the sigh of tree branches
and the rustle of leaves,
the ocean's ceaseless pull,
the unnameable ache of emotions
stirred by wordless song.
Ancient, instinctive,
it hums beneath the clamor of the everyday.

We're schooled to dwell in the rational —
to measure, strategize, control.
These are tools, sharp and necessary —
but frail sovereigns.

When life frays,
when identity falters,
when old ways crumble,
logic alone cannot hold.
We need a richer tongue.

Mythology offers this —
not solutions, but bearings;
not facts, but guidance.

As Joseph Campbell taught,
myth is no falsehood — it's a metaphor,
a bridge to truths beyond the visible,
felt in the bones before named by the mind.

You don't turn to myths for distraction.
You turn to them to recall.
To see that the turmoil you face
may weave into a larger tapestry.

To know that fear, loss, or longing
aren't character's flaws —
they're doorways.
To understand that your trials
mark not a wrong turn,
but a step into hallowed ground.

The mythic mind doesn't seek
to unravel life's enigma.
It seeks to meet it — with awe.

And in that meeting, something stirs.
You glimpse the threads beneath your struggles.
You hear the summons hidden in upheaval.
You sense your story as a fragment
of a vast, ancient narrative —
still unfolding, far from complete.

As you journey through these chapters,
let your mythic mind awaken.
It will guide you not to answers,
but to questions that illuminate your path.

Myths as Blueprints for the Psyche

Every myth is a mirror —
reflecting not the outer world,
but the unseen depths within.

Before psychology gave names to our inner workings,
myths clothed the subconscious in vivid imagery.

They gave form to suppressed fears,
unspoken desires,
buried strengths,
and lingering wounds.

What we now diagram with theories and charts,
ancient cultures wove into deities, quests, and signs.

When Persephone descends to the underworld,
it's more than a tale of seasons —
it's the soul's plunge into its own shadows.
When Odysseus wanders, island to island,
it's not just a journey home —
it's the psyche caught
in distraction, temptation, delay.
When the Buddha rests beneath the Bodhi tree,
unswayed by illusion or dread,
it's not merely a spiritual dawn —
it's the quiet center of every human awakening.

These are not relics of a bygone age.
They are blueprints of the psyche,
revealing the mechanics of transformation —
not in distant tales,
but within the crucible of your own being.

Carl Jung named these patterns *archetypes* —
timeless motifs etched deep in the human spirit,
transcending era or culture.

The Hero's courage.
The Trickster's cunning.
The Shadow's hidden truths.
The Wise Elder's guidance.
The Anima's inner balance.

We don't create these figures —
we uncover them, alive within us.

This is the enduring gift of myth:
it doesn't just captivate —
it unveils.
It lights the hidden scaffolding of the soul,
showing us the contours of our inner world.

Myths rise most vividly in times of fracture
or change —
when old identities crack,
when familiar frames no longer hold.
In those moments, the psyche reaches
for a deeper language,
often finding it in story.

Not to solve the chaos,
but to navigate it.
To make meaning of the dark,
to remind you that others have walked this path.

Myth becomes more than narrative —
it becomes a guide.

A quiet voice that nudges you on:
Yes, this road is daunting.
Yes, it feels like an ending.
But press forward.
This is the way through —
and you are not alone.

These archetypal patterns don't exist in isolation.
They pulse through the stories
your culture tells about what life means.

Cultural Stories, Personal Journeys

The tales that move through your world
carry more than entertainment.
They shape how you see yourself.

Every culture spins its tales,
and every soul — knowingly or not —
moves within their resonance.

Your beliefs about love, sacrifice, ambition, fate —
they don't spring from thin air.
They're inherited,
absorbed through the stories that surround you,
shaped by the myths that hum
beneath the surface of your world.

The arc of fall and redemption.
The clash of light against shadow.
The lure of a chosen destiny.
The peril of forbidden truths.
The rise of the unlikely victor.

These echo in bedtime tales,
pulse through films,
shape rituals,
sway convictions.

They form the unseen lens
through which we interpret human experience —
not because they were imposed,
but because the culture made them *feel* true.

Yet while these stories belong to the collective,
your journey is singular and personal.
You don't need to name a myth to inhabit it.

When betrayal forces you to choose
between closing your heart or mending it —
you are in a myth.
When you stand torn between duty and desire —
you are in a myth.
When a quiet call urges you to leave the familiar
for an uncertain horizon —
you are in a myth.

Myths transcend eras and borders.
Gilgamesh grieved and sought meaning
in ancient Sumer.
Arjuna wavered on the battlefield,
weighing duty against compassion in the Gita's verses.
Inanna braved the underworld's depths.
Moses wandered the desert's expanse.

And so do you —
in your own way,
in your own skin.

These stories endure because they are not just theirs.
They are yours.
Your struggles, your crossroads, your leaps —
they are not random.
They are chapters in a narrative
you didn't realize you were weaving.

Seeing this shifts everything.
Your pain gains purpose.
Your choices gain weight.
You are not just living —
you are crafting a story.
And now, aware of the myths you carry,
you hold the pen to shape what comes next.

The Hidden Power of Symbols

Before words bound our thoughts,
symbols carried meaning.
A circle was more than the sun —
it evoked eternity, unity, the arc of existence.
A serpent was no mere creature —
it signaled renewal, peril, transformation.

We still speak this language,
though we rarely notice.

A ring binds vows to forever.
A candle's flame holds memory's glow.
A cap and gown mark a rite of passage and
crossing into new realms.
These acts are ancient —
their resonance is timeless.

Symbols render the unseen tangible.
They give form to what words cannot hold —
sorrow, devotion, aspiration, transcendence.

In myths, symbols don't adorn the tale —
they drive it.

The forest is no mere backdrop —
it's the uncharted.
The beast is not just danger —
it's your hidden self.
The sword is not just a weapon —
it's the will you sharpen through choice.
The treasure isn't only gold and coins —
it's the insight and wisdom you'll earn,
if you're brave enough to face what guards it.
The threshold is not merely a doorway —
it's the moment you shed who you were.

Today's stories carry these echoes,
often unwittingly.
A lightsaber is more than a blade —
it's a mantle of purpose.
A red pill is no simple choice —
it's an awakening.
Superhero capes and emblems
are modern sigils and symbolic shorthand
for archetypes as old as time.

This is why certain tales grip us.
Not for their novelty —
but for their deep familiarity.

They stir a quiet recognition,
an unnameable pull.
When a film, a novel, a melody
moves you without reason,
you've brushed a symbol —
not culture's, but yours.

To see your life through a symbolic lens
is to unlock a new vision.

You move beyond the surface —
the job, the loss, the bank statement —
and begin to ask:
What does this moment reveal?
What truth does it point toward?
What is seeking to unfold?

Transformation isn't born from dissecting life
like data.
It arises from tracing the symbolic threads
woven through your days —
and daring to follow where they may lead.

When Life Stops Making Sense

There comes a time —
sudden or gradual —
when the narrative you've lived by
crumbles.

It might follow a wound:
a loss that cuts deep,
a trust betrayed,
a vision that fades to ash.

Or it might creep in slowly —
a gnawing unease,
the sense that your carefully built world
feels like a cage with no breath.

You reach for answers.
You retrace old plans,
lean harder into what once anchored you —
work, approval, control.
But nothing holds.
You drift, unmoored.

This is not collapse.
This is awakening.
The old story must unravel
for a new one to take root.

Yet our world offers little wisdom
for this liminal space.
It urges you to press on,
to stay bright,
to drown the ache in busyness or consumption.
But what you hunger for
is *meaning*.

In ancient times, myths held this void.
They gave chaos a shape —
a symbolic frame that whispered:
This descent is not your end.
It's your rite of passage

Rituals cradled grief.
Symbols wove transformation.
Stories made pain a chapter, not a verdict.

Today, we have tools — therapy, books, voices online.
They help, yet often lack the mythic pulse.
When life fractures,
you may feel alone in the wreckage,
as if your disarray were a flaw —
not a universal crossing.

But mythology speaks differently.
It declares every loss a threshold,
every exile a seed of return.
When life ceases to cohere,
it's not a sign of your failing —
it's a signal that something deeper stirs.

This is the space between tales.
And it is hallowed.
No map awaits you here,
only silence,
uncertainty,
exposure.
And yet — possibility.

Here, the old self softens its hold.
The symbolic mind rekindles.
The myth begins to draw you in —
not from ancient pages,
but from the quiet within.
As you stand in this in-between,
you're not lost.
You're beginning.

Awakening the Myth Within

You were not born merely to endure.
You were born to become.

Becoming is not about refining a surface self —
it's about unveiling the deeper truth beneath.
It's seeing that your life is no random string of days,
but a tapestry woven with meaning —
if you dare to view it so.

Mythology is more than a lens for understanding.
It's a call.
Not to analyze ancient tales,
but to live with mythic awareness.

To see your life as a sacred story,
not a ledger of events.
To notice the patterns that return —
the fears that linger,
the longings that pull,
the trials that test —
and to ask what they signify.
To stop viewing pain as a wrong turn,
and instead see it as a signpost.

This perspective is not fantasy.
It's depth.
It reveals that the currents of your outer world
mirror the tides within your soul —
that every challenge carries
the seed of transformation.

The myths you'll meet in these pages —
and those you've carried,
perhaps unknowingly, all along —
are not relics to admire.

They are sparks to ignite you.
They remind you
that you're not merely weathering life —
you're navigating a path.
A path trodden by countless before,
yet shaped uniquely by your steps.

As you stand at this chapter's close,
a new beginning takes form —
not only in this book,
but within you.

The way forward may be unclear,
yet a quiet knowing vibrates within.
The myth was never apart from you —
it has been waiting for you to claim it.

Turn the page with this truth:
You are not stepping into theory —
you are entering sacred ground.

The Hero's Journey is no distant framework.
It is your story, waiting to be claimed.
The map is ancient.
The journey is yours.
The next step is calling.

~

3

THE HERO'S JOURNEY

You've sensed it all along —
that unsettling feeling,
a pull beneath the rhythm of your days.

No matter how polished your life appears,
something deeper beckons.
Something quieter yet more urgent.
Something essential.
And truer.

It may not yet feel like a "call to adventure."
It might be a restless ache,
a tension between who you are
and who you're meant to become.
A sign that something essential is missing —
not in the world around you,
but within your own depths.

This is where the *Hero's Journey* begins.
Not with epic quests or celestial signs,
but with an inner shift.
A quiet awakening.
A question you can no longer ignore.

Joseph Campbell devoted his life to charting this arc
across myths, cultures, and time.
What he uncovered was no mere template for tales —
it was a reflection of the human soul's path.

Across continents and centuries,
from ancient epics to sacred rites,
he traced a universal rhythm:
departure from the known,
trials in the uncharted,
and return, transformed.

The power of this journey lies
not in its shared thread,
but in its intimacy and personal relevance.
You are too on this path —
whether you chose it or not,
whether you see it yet or not.

Campbell's revelation wasn't that some lives
are more heroic —
it was that every transformation
follows a hidden structure.

From the odes of ancient Greece
to the parables of the East,
from indigenous ceremonies to modern stories,
the same archetype emerges.
It's not bound by culture —
it's woven into the human spirit.
A mythic imprint
that lives inside the human condition itself.

This is the Hero's Journey —
not a flight of fancy,
but a map of the soul's becoming.
You may already be walking it,
unaware of the pattern beneath your steps.

Not because you were handed a guide,
but because the urge to grow,
to break free,
to become wholly yourself
is etched in your being.

What follows is not only dramatic theory.
It's a mirror —
revealing that your struggles,
your questions,
your thresholds
are part of a story older than your own.
To see this pattern is to shift your gaze —
and in that shift,
the journey ahead begins to unfold.

The Story Written in All of Us

We often believe our lives are ours to forge —
each choice, each sorrow,
each turning point uniquely our own.
But what if your path follows an ancient design?
What if the shape of your journey
has been passed on through ages,
etched in stories across time?

Joseph Campbell sought not to invent
an academic theory,
but to unravel a mystery:
why tales from distant lands —
a Greek warrior's odyssey,
an Indian prince's quest,
a Polynesian daughter's voyage —
share a common pulse.
This shared pulse reveals an ancient pattern.

Departure.
Initiation.
Return.

Not a rigid line,
but a living spiral —
beginning when the familiar world
no longer holds you.
It draws you into uncharted realms

of challenge, doubt, and growth,
then guides you back —
transformed, carrying new wisdom.

You've felt this arc in stories that linger:
Luke Skywalker abandoning Tatooine,
Neo choosing the red pill,
Moana venturing beyond the reef.
Each hears the call.
Each hesitates.
Each braves the unknown.
Each returns bearing gifts the world needs.

Why do these stories grip us?
They echo a truth buried within —
that you, too, are called.
Beyond fear,
beyond resistance,
beyond the upheaval of change,
lies purpose.

These tales resonate
because they reveal
what we already instinctively know:
transformation is our birthright.

The Hero's Journey is more than a template.
It's a trace of the soul's imprint,
yours included.

We don't cherish these stories for their novelty,
but for their recognition of us.
They show what it feels like to be human —
of what it means to stand at a threshold,
to falter,
to be broken open and reshaped by trials,
and to emerge transformed.

This is the sacred rhythm:

Departure — the moment life asks more of you,
ready or not.
Initiation — the crucible of tests and truths
that carve your inner strength.
Return — the weaving of your growth
into the fabric of the world.

This is not just plain narrative.
It's the soul work of becoming.
These stories move you
because their pattern already lives within you —
as a truth waiting to be reclaimed.

As you step forward,
know that this ancient rhythm
waits to guide your unfolding path.

But how does this rhythm begin?
How does the call first find you?

The Universal Call to Adventure

The call rarely arrives with fanfare.
No heralded summons.
No glowing sword.
No sage at your threshold.

More often, it's a quiet unease —
a subtle discord,
a sense that the life you've shaped
no longer holds the contours of your emerging self.

The Call to Adventure is seldom clear at first.
It may surface as an unnameable restlessness,
a dream that lingers at the edge of thought,
or a weariness cloaked in exhaustion, loss, or doubt.
A question may haunt you:
Is this the sum of my days?

Reflect on your own moments —
when life demanded more,
pushed you beyond the familiar,
urged you toward the uncharted.
These are your calls to adventure.

And life will call you —
it already has.

It heeds no borders,
no age,
no past.
It speaks to all,
relentless, impartial,
offering trials to forge your resilience,
chances veiled as uncertainty,
moments to awaken your hidden strength.

The call's gift is its intimacy —
it speaks in the tongue you're poised to hear.

Sometimes it roars.
More often, it whispers.
Yet when it comes,
something within you shifts —
a quiet knowing
that you're meant for something truer,
more aligned,
more alive.

You need not chase distant horizons to hear it.
The call can find you in a crowded room,
amid the hum of routine,
or in the stillness of a fleeting glance.
It's not the outer world shifting —
it's your inner self stirring,
refusing to remain dormant.

From your first breath,
you've been on this path.
Every wound endured,
every hope pursued,
every fracture,
every triumph —
all weave the threads of your singular story.

Yet its pattern is timeless.
You may tread quiet trails of self-discovery,
climb steep peaks of ambition,
or navigate the depths of sorrow.
You may wander, question, unravel —
only to rise reshaped.

These are not purported missteps.
They are the journey.
What you first saw as barriers
were invitations disguised —
to grow,
to awaken,
to become.

This is no abstract idea —
it's your roadmap.
A guide for those ready to step beyond
the safety of the known,
to face the mystery of the unknown
with courage and resolve.

You were not meant to linger in another's shadow.
You were meant to carve your own way,
to become, time and again,
the self you've always held within.

You don't have to know where it's leading.
You only need to answer the call.

Recognizing Your Call

Pause here.
Look back at your own life.

When did you last feel that restless pull?
What dreams have you been postponing?
What part of your current life
feels too small for who you're becoming?

The call speaks in whispers before it roars.

It might be:
A career that no longer fits.
A relationship asking for deeper truth.
A creative urge you've been silencing.
A wound that's ready to heal.
A fear that's revealed to be faced.

Write down what comes to mind.
Don't judge it.
Just witness what rises.

The Refusal: Why We Resist Our Own Becoming

We dream of transformation —
in the abstract, it shines.
But when the call arrives,
we falter.
This hesitation springs from our humanity.

The unknown unsettles,
its edges sharp.
Even a life that chafes,
constricting as it is,
feels known —
and the known cloaks itself in safety,
however much it confines.

So we pause.
We reason away the urge.
We smother the summons
with duties, diversions, careful justifications.

The timing isn't right, we say.
We're unprepared.
Surely others are better suited
to claim a life more vibrant.
Perhaps this half-fit existence
is enough.

This is the *Refusal of the Call* —
not a failure,
but a chapter in the journey.
Even in myth, heroes hesitate.

Simba flees the Pride Lands.
Harry Potter questions his place at Hogwarts.
Katniss steps forward,
yet wrestles with obligation and fear.
Moana, bound to the sea,
recoils when its waves surge too fiercely.

These are not detours from destiny —
they are doorways,
revealing what must be met:
doubt,
shame,
the weight of others' expectations.

You may feel this pull too.
You may dread what you must release —
bonds, identities,
the stories you've clung to for control.
You may wonder if it's too late,
if you're too broken,
too flawed to step forward.

But hesitation is not unreadiness.
It's the sign you stand at a true threshold.
What matters is not how long you linger,
but whether you face the truth of why.

Transformation demands a price.
No awakening comes
without letting go of what was.

The call's terror lies not in what you might become,
but in what you must leave behind.

Yet if you feel its tug,
even through the fear,
you're already further than you know.
The journey is not waiting for you to be ready —
it's waiting for you to take the first step.

Ask yourself:
Where do you feel resistance?
What stories do you tell yourself
about why "now isn't the time"?

Name your hesitations.
They're not obstacles —
they're gateways to understanding
what matters most.

Redefining the Hero

The word *hero* carries an old weight —
a figure clad in armor,
blade raised,
marching alone into epic strife.

For ages,
heroism has been cast in conquest,
etched in tales of kings,
stoic warriors,
lone adventurers crossing perilous lands.
But that vision captures only a fragment of the truth.

Here, in this journey,
we release that narrow frame.

True heroism is more than battle cries
and flawless triumphs.
It transcends gender, tradition, or expectations.
It seeks no spotlight,
craves no crown.
It's courage.
It's transformation.
It's the resolve to face your depths —
and grow through them.

Hero is not a badge to earn.
It's a call to answer —
a spark within you that defies surrender,
that rises, again and again,
even when the world bids you stay small.

The hero is the one who shows up —
for others and for their own becoming.

This journey belongs to you,
no matter your origin or unique path.

It is a story for all —
survivors, dreamers, healers, rebels, seekers, lovers.
For anyone brave enough to evolve.

Your battles may not gleam with steel,
no arrows, no dragons,
but they are no less real.
They are doubts that gnaw,
griefs that linger,
shame that clings,
hope that falters.
The foes you face may not roar —
they whisper,
they mutter,
yet their weight is crushing.
And so is the strength they forge.

To be a hero is not to evade the fall —
it is to rise from it.
Not because you lack fear,
but because you know you're meant for more.

Your journey will not mirror another's —
nor should it.
But the rhythm endures:
the call,
the descent,
the trial,
the return.
Each stage etched not in myth,
but in your breath,
your scars,
your ascendance.

Cast aside the mold of what a hero *should* be.
Shatter it.
Step forward not with certainty,
but with resolve.
Let these words guide you —
but never confine you.

Your life is not a script imposed upon you.
It's a story unfolding through you.
This is your call.
Your adventure.
Your moment to begin.
Will you answer it?

Your Journey Awaits

You don't need to map every turn of the path
to take the first step.
All you need as awareness —
of the unease that stirs,
the yearning that persists,
the quiet resolve that surfaces
when you thought you had none left.

The call doesn't echo from some distant shore.
It wells up from within —
a gentle, unyielding summons
rising from your depths.

Follow the thread you've felt all along.
It may be faint, tangled, or half-forgotten,
but it's there, woven into your days,
guiding you toward what's true.

Right now, in this moment:
What is one small action
that will honor the call you feel?

It might be:
A conversation you've been avoiding.
A dream you've been dismissing.
A boundary you've been afraid to set.
A risk you've been postponing.

Choose one.
Not tomorrow.
Today.

The Hero's Journey doesn't begin
with certainty or spectacle —
it begins with the courage
to answer what's calling you now.

4

THE DEPARTURE — ANSWERING THE CALL

The journey starts long before the first step.
It begins with a tremor —
a quiet unease,
faint at first,
then unyielding.
A whisper of discontent.
A pull that calls:
There is more to you than this

The Hero's Journey names this stage
the **Departure** —
not for the act of leaving,
but for the courage to release.

It's rarely clear at the outset.
It may rise in the lifeless weight of a routine,
in the hollow pause of a bond grown thin,
or crash through in a moment of upheaval —
a loss,
a betrayal,
a fracture that upends what you knew.
Sometimes, it lingers —
a subtle ache,
a yearning for something truer,
more vital,
more alive.

The call is always the same:
Step beyond the familiar.
Trade the safety of the known
for the promise of transformation.

Yet, like every hero in tales across time,
we pause.
We resist.
We weave excuses:
I'm too far along to change course.
What if I falter?
I'm not prepared.
I'm not enough.

This refusal is no fatal flaw —
it's the first trial of your transformation.
A mirror revealing
our fears,
our habits,
the narratives we've gripped too tightly.

But when we cease fleeing,
when we dare to face the possibility of change —
something shifts.
Guidance emerges from the darkness.

In myth, the hero receives supernatural aid.
In our world, it's often more modest:
a mentor's wisdom,
a friend's presence,
a teacher's insight,
or a book that arrives precisely when needed.

They don't tread the path for us —
they light the way
when our courage wavers.

Now comes the threshold —
the point of no return.
The quiet *yes* that alters all.

Joseph Campbell called this the *Belly of the Whale* —
the symbolic surrender of the old self.
Once crossed, the past recedes.
The former you no longer fits.
You stand in the unknown —
raw,
exposed,
yet already reshaping.

The Departure is more than leaving behind.
It's the daring to let go of who you were
to embrace who you are becoming.
Here, this essential process finds its first foothold.

A Note on Structure

The Hero's Journey weaves through three vital arcs:
1. Departure — stepping away from the familiar.
2. Initiation — braving the uncharted.
3. Return — reentering your world, transformed.

In the chapters ahead,
you'll find sections marked accordingly:
1.1 (in Chapter 4), 2.1 (in Chapter 5), 3.1 (in Chapter 6),
and so on.

However, this is no rigid instructions manual.
It's a compass —
crafted not for rote learning,
but for soul-deep discovery.

A guide not for linear understanding —
but for inner exploration.
One that invites you to trace your own path
through the terrain of the larger human journey.

1.1 The Ordinary World: Comfort vs. Stagnation

Every journey begins in the realm of the familiar —
or the *Ordinary World*.
Here, life feels steady and safe,
its patterns are predictable.
You know the cadence,
the roles,
the boundaries.
There's structure.
There's comfort.
And often, the illusion of certainty.

Yet beneath this calm,
a quiet unease takes root —
a subtle ache,
a whisper that lingers:
Is this all there is?

The Ordinary World isn't inherently bad.
It serves a purpose.
It grounds you,
offers roots to stand firm,
space to function, to belong.

But left unexamined,
this haven becomes a cage.
When ease calcifies into complacency,
when routine dulls to inertia,
the spirit begins to fade.

You may have a role that sustains you,
a bond that shines outwardly,
a rhythm that leaves little room for doubt.

Yet something vital slips away —
the piece of you sidelined,
muted,
or surrendered
to meet expectations,
to stay secure,
to blend in.

This is your starting point.
And certainly far from your destination.
It's the soil where seeds of change will first germinate,
waiting for you to notice
and choose to let it grow.

Why This Stage Matters

This stage isn't about casting blame
or upending your life in haste.
It's about awakening.

Transformation begins
when you dare to feel the unease —
not by burying it,
not by explaining it away,
but by meeting it with clear eyes.

The change rarely sprouts from action alone.
It takes root in truth —
a quiet, unflinching moment
where you ask:
What have I surrendered for this sense of safety?
What part of my soul have I muted
to keep the surface smooth?

This honesty is the first spark,
lighting the path to who you're meant to become.

Key Insight

The Ordinary World isn't your captor.
It's silencing the yearning for something deeper
that dims your spirit.
Comfort alone doesn't confine —
evading truth builds the cage.

Self-Reflection: The Terrain of the Known

Pause to map the landscape of your inner world
with these questions, crafted for honest reckoning:

Where do you feel tethered, dulled, or adrift?
Which habits still sustain you —
and which quietly sap your energy?
What truths within you have you hushed
to preserve the illusion of normalcy?
What aspirations have you set out of reach —
and what might it take to claim them now?

Let these inquiries be keys,
unlocking not blame,
but insight.

Action Step:
Create a Snapshot of Your Ordinary World

Open your journal.
Sketch a circle and name it:
My Ordinary World.
Within it, capture the pillars of your life today —
your work, home, bonds, habits, beliefs, routines.

Next to each, pause and reflect:
What nourishes life — vibrant, aligned, true?
What rests in balance —
neither draining nor uplifting?
What weighs heavy, confines,
or no longer fits your truth?

This is not a call to judge.
It's a pursuit of unflinching clarity.
By mapping the contours of your now,
you begin to envision what might yet unfold.
To shape a new path,
you must first see the ground beneath your feet.

From Spark to Story

The journey doesn't launch with bold declarations.
It starts with a quiet resolve —
the courage to voice what hums within:
Something in me yearns for more.

That whisper, however soft,
is the ember.
From it,
your awakening lights up.

1.2 The Call to Adventure: Recognizing the Spark

Every true transformation begins with a jolt —
the *Call to Adventure.*
It doesn't always erupt like a crisis.
Sometimes it's a pause —
a stark realization
that the life you've built
no longer feels like yours.

The comfort of the Ordinary World
starts to choke.
Something raw inside you surges —
demanding more.

It might flare as a nagging thought —
sharp, vivid,
impossible to dismiss.
An idea that won't let go.
A vision that burns through your defenses.
A hunger that haunts you,
no matter how you try to ignore it.

Or it might hit like a storm —
a loss that upends you,
a betrayal that cuts,
a diagnosis that shatters your rhythm,
leaving nowhere to hide.

Whatever its shape, the message is still the same:
Your old world is too small.
A larger one beckons.

It arrives without a guidebook.
It offers no guarantees.
Only a doorway —
and the dare to step through.

Deep down, past fear and doubt,
you do know:
You can't stay put.
A truer life awaits.
It's time to rise.

Why This Stage Matters

The call doesn't always feel grand.
It often arrives as discomfort —
a subtle and nagging sense
that something vital is absent,
that your world,
though intact on the outside,
no longer fits the shape of your soul.

You might find yourself imagining a different life,
reaching for dreams you thought long buried,
or sensing the gap between who you are
and the role you've been playing.

It's unsettling.
It's disruptive.
And yes — it's daunting.
But it is also sacred.

This is the spark of your becoming —
not born of clarity,
but of a longing too fierce to dismiss.

Key Insight
The call to adventure seeks not perfection —
but openness.
No need to hold every answer.
Simply heed
the truth your life is already revealing.

The Sacred Inconvenience

The call may not arrive on your terms.
It often strikes when you're least prepared —
when life feels too full,
too tangled,
too unsteady for change.
You may feel swamped,
adrift in doubt,
irritated by its timing,
unsettled by its jolt.

But these feelings aren't reasons for panic or despair.
They're signs of awakening.

The call doesn't seek to disrupt for disruption's sake.
It arrives to rouse you —
to draw you toward a life
you might have convinced yourself to never pursue.

It's not a punishment,
but an invitation —
a subtle nudge toward the truth
you've been circling,
urging you to step into the fullness
of who you're meant to be.

Identifying Your Call

To recognize the call,
you must learn to listen —
not to the noise of the world,
but to the voice within.

Pause and answer:
Where does your heart drift when the noise fades?
What dreams lie buried beneath duty or dread?
What corners of your life feel cramped, lifeless,
or out of sync?

Your call may sound as a yearning for work
that matters.
A drive to mend what lingers unhealed.
A craving for bonds that run deeper.
It might spark as a creative urge,
a pull toward a new place or pace,
or the fierce need to honor yourself first.

These aren't fleeting whims.
They are dispatches from your truest self —
beacons urging you toward growth.
Not mere disruptions.
But invitations to grow.

The Power of Discomfort

Discomfort sharpens your view of what's true.
It rises when your inner world
begins to outgrow your outer reality.
Rather than recoil,
meet its unyielding force head-on.

The unease before a daring leap.
The drag of repetitive days.
The strain threading through your closest ties.
These aren't ruptures.
They're breakthroughs in disguise.

When your core outgrows its bounds,
your world feels tight —
off-balance,
hard to define.

That friction isn't failure.
It's the unrelenting tension daring you:
Stay tethered to the known —
or reach for growth?

Listening to Your Intuition

In a world thick with doubt and distraction,
intuition is your North Star.
It doesn't always shout.
But it never deceives.

Unlike fear, which tightens and binds,
intuition feels open, clear, expansive —
a calm certainty that settles deep.
It doesn't demand.
It beckons.

You can hone it through stillness —
journaling, solitude, moments in nature.
Times when the noise fades,
letting your inner voice rise.

When something lands true,
resonating in your core —
firm, unforced, undeniable —
that's your call speaking through you.

Answering the Call

The call doesn't always blaze with spectacle.
Sometimes it's a faint, persistent question
that clings to your thoughts.
Sometimes it's a fracture —
unwanted, yet necessary.

You might see it in:
A job that no longer inspires you.
A role that's lost its fire.
A deep ache for love, purpose, or truth.
A spiritual awakening you don't yet understand.
A heartbreak, a loss, a shift you didn't seek —
yet can't turn away from.

To ignore the call is to cling to safety over daring —
but the price is steep.
Unheeded yearnings don't fade.
They simmer,
morphing into bitterness, regret, or exhaustion.

But when you respond —
even with a trembling voice —
the world tilts.
You align with the truth of your potential.
You declare to existence:
I'm here.
I'm ready to become.

Action Step: Acknowledge the Call

Pause today to face what's been rising within you.
Ask:
What's been tugging at my edges lately?
Where am I being called to evolve, pivot, or start anew?
What have I been pushing away —
and what could unfold if I finally said yes?

Write without restraint.
No editing.
No refining.
Truth doesn't demand perfection —
it only asks to be heard.

The Moment of Choice

Your call has already sounded.
It may have been a fleeting thought.
It may have struck with force.
But if these words resonate,
a part of you is poised to respond.

The Call to Adventure offers
no guarantees of comfort.
It offers meaning.
It doesn't demand you forsake yourself —
but urges you to embrace
who you were born to become.

One question remains:
Will you step forward?

1.3 Refusal of the Call: The Fear That Holds Us Back

No hero strides fearlessly into the unknown.
After the call's first spark
comes a wave of resistance —
a hesitant pause,
or a fierce rejection rising from within.

When growth beckons,
instinct recoils.
Fear sharpens its edge.
Reason argues for caution.
Doubt creeps in,
and the comfort of the known
grows nearly irresistible.

Am I truly prepared?
Is this the right time?
What if I stumble?

This is the *Refusal of the Call* —
not a failure of courage,
but a deeply human moment of reckoning.
It's your mind shielding you.
It's your ego bracing itself.
It's the primal urge to see change as peril —
and predictability as refuge.

Yet growth demands more.
Resistance, though natural,
is not the story's end.
It's the edge of transformation,
where courage begins to get a voice.

Why This Stage Matters

Refusing the call isn't a flaw.
It's only human.
This is when your former self grips tightest —
not out of inadequacy,
but out of fear.

Fear of what you must release.
Fear of who you might become.

The refusal is your mind's shield —
a reflex to guard against risk,
uncertainty,
and loss.
Transformation requires a kind of surrender —
not of life,
but of the self you've known.

Even if the familiar feels hollow,
it is still certain.
The unknown, however bright its promise,
looms as a threat.

So you pause.
You justify.
You cling to what's known,
even as it grows cramped,
constraining,
distant from the truth of who you're called to be.

Understanding the Fear

To step forward,
you must first name what holds you back.
Is it the sting of failure?
The weight of being seen — and judged?
The dread of letting others down?
Or yourself?
Or perhaps it's success itself —
and the demands it might bring.

Whatever its shape,
fear demands recognition.
You cannot transform what you refuse to confront.

It hides behind many faces:
Procrastination, disguised as waiting
for the perfect moment.
Perfectionism, posing as unpreparedness.
Overthinking, dressed as pragmatism.
Ceaseless *busyness*,
dodging the stillness that would reveal your true call.

Beneath each mask lies a deeper truth:
the hunger for a life that matters.
You wouldn't feel fear
if you weren't standing at the edge
of something meaningful.

Fear is often misread.
We see it as a red flag — a signal of danger,
urging retreat.
But not all fear is the same.

There's the primal kind —
a shield against true harm.
Then there's the fear that surges
when you stand at the edge of transformation,
a new chapter,
a daring leap.
A change that could redefine who you are.

This fear doesn't shout *Stop!*
It demands focus.
It signals you're nearing something essential.

Many believe that what truly matters
would feel effortless,
certain,
fearless.

But the deepest truths often come
with trembling hands
and a racing heart.
Fear is the proof
you've ventured beyond the familiar,
into the territory of real growth.

When fear arises, ask:
Am I truly at risk?
Or am I simply stretched by change?
If it's the latter —
press on.
The unease isn't a command to turn back.
It's part of becoming.

Sometimes, discovering who you are
means facing what scares you most —
not recklessly,
but with purpose.
Courage isn't fear's absence.
It's the choice to move forward —
because the stakes are so high.

Key Insight

Fear isn't a warning to retreat —
it's a marker of something vital ahead.
Not an obstacle, but a threshold.
When you stop fighting it,
fear no longer obscures the way —
it begins to light it.

Challenging Limiting Beliefs

Every fear rests on a belief —
often not your own,
but borrowed.
Handed down through family, culture, or chance,
shaped by others' doubts and trepidations.
It might echo as an inner refrain:
I'm too far along to begin anew.
I lack what's needed.
Lives like that aren't meant for someone like me.

These aren't facts.
They're inherited notions —
and notions can be tested.
They hold sway only if left unchallenged.

Pause and probe:
Where did this conviction take root?
Is it grounded in reality — or merely familiar?
Who could I become if I set it aside?

This is the spark of rebellion.
Swapping a confining belief
for one that empowers is a bold stand —
a rejection of limits born from others' fears.

This is where your story pivots:
From stuck — to possible.
From merely enduring — to trusting yourself.
From restraint — to claiming your own power.

This is how you craft a new chapter —
one where you are capable,
resilient,
and free to forge your truest self.

The Cost of Inaction

Every choice carries a price —
even the choice to stand still.
Ignoring the call may seem safer now,
but safety exacts its own toll over time.

What starts as caution
can calcify into regret.
Unheeded desires don't vanish —
they sink beneath the surface,
turning into silent sorrows.

The dreams left unpursued.
The potential left dormant.
The what-ifs that grow heavier
with each passing day.

Ask yourself with care:
What possibilities might slip away if I don't act now?
What will my life be in a year if I stay unchanged?
How will it feel to look back —
and wonder what might have been?

The mind often dwells on the dangers of change,
but rarely names the weight of staying put.
When you weigh both —
action against inaction,
a new clarity begins to emerge.

Not the absence of fear,
but the rise of something stronger:
Readiness.
Determination.
A deep certainty
that the ache of stagnation
now outweighs the dread of stepping forward.

Self-Reflection Exercise

Take a quiet moment.
Find a space to simply be — and breathe.

This is no judgment.
It's a call to meet your truest self.
Let your thoughts flow freely,
unafraid of what they might reveal.

Journal your responses to these questions:

What fear anchors you in place right now?
Not the fleeting worry —
but the deeper dread
you rarely voice.

What limiting belief still binds you —
and is it truly yours?
Trace its roots.
Whose words does it carry?
Does it still fit who you are?

If your path stays unchanged,
where will you stand in a year?
Not just in place —
but in heart,
in connection,
in spirit.

Now imagine choosing courage over ease —
what might your life become?

Let the vision unfold.
Not in perfect strokes —
but in possibility.
Write what rises.
Write what moves you.
Begin exactly where you are.

Action Step: Reclaim Your Power

This is where real transformation begins —
not with a grand gesture,
but with a single, intentional act.

1. Name your fear.
Write it plainly.
Be precise.
Fear grows in shadows —
once defined, its hold begins to weaken.
2. Test it.
Ask: *Is this rooted in truth — or habit?*
Whose voice speaks here?
What if the opposite held equal weight?
3. Act small, but bold.
Take one defiant step to break the old pattern.
Reach out to the mentor.
Sign up for the course.
Voice the truth you've kept buried.
Even a single move toward what daunts you
claims and builds your strength.

The aim isn't to feel prepared.
It's to move forward — fear and all.

Beyond the Threshold

Refusal is not a defeat.
It's a crossroads.

It's life challenging you —
How fiercely do you crave this change?

This is the crucible where truth takes shape.
Each step through fear —
tentative,
raw,
imperfect —
carves you closer to the hero you're meant to be.

Don't wait for fear to fade.
Carry it with you.
Let it walk beside you,
not as a captor,
but as a companion to your courage.

Beyond the resistance
beams the self you're meant to become.

1.4 Meeting the Mentor: Finding Guidance on the Path

No hero treads the journey alone.
The path is yours —
intimate, singular —
yet never wholly solitary.
At critical junctures —
when fear clamps down,
when doubt drowns out hope —
a mentor emerges.

Sometimes they're clear:
a seasoned teacher,
a knowing guide,
someone who's walked the terrain.
Other times, they appear unexpected —
a friend's steady presence,
a challenge that sharpens you,
a stranger's kindness,
or a single phrase that lingers,
etched in your mind long after it's spoken.

Their arrival carries one truth:
You're not meant to face this alone.

Mentors don't take your steps for you —
they light the way forward.
They offer clarity when your thoughts blur,
courage when your spirit falters,
tools, inspiring tales, or questions
precisely when you need them.
They share strength when yours wavers,
and vision when fear narrows your sight.

In every myth,
there comes a moment
when the mentor meets the hero's gaze
and delivers the truth you didn't know you needed:
You are enough.
You are ready.

Why This Stage Matters

Meeting the mentor marks a turning point —
not because they rescue you,
but because they recognize you.
They don't offer a map.
They kindle your trust in your own compass —
your capacity to navigate the way.

Mentors don't bestow strength —
they reveal the fire already within you,
flickering beneath doubt.

They hold up a mirror,
showing you the self you've yet to claim,
the potential you've overlooked
in moments of reluctance or fog.
Their presence is a reminder:
You are not alone in this.
Their words, their challenge, their faith,
reawaken your own.
They don't walk your path —
they help you see it clearly,
equipping you to step forward
with the courage that was yours all along.

Mentors Take Many Forms

Mentors don't always arrive draped in wisdom
or wielding grand revelations.

Often, they slip into your life quietly,
woven into the fabric of ordinary moments:

A line from a film,
a song lyric you've known forever —
suddenly sharp with new meaning.
A conversation that tilts your view of the world.
A book's passage that strikes like a spark.
A coach who sees the you
you're still daring to trust.
A setback that reveals what ease obscures.

Mentors wear countless faces —
people, stories, experiences, even fleeting dreams.
Yet they share one mark:
They ignite something within you,
rousing the courage and clarity
already waiting to rise.

Recognizing Your Mentors

Mentors surround you —
if you open your eyes to them.
Not every guide wears a title or a gown.
Some arrive unassuming —
through a moment's clarity, a brief encounter,
or a truth that endures.

Reflect:
Whose words echo in my mind,
resonating long after they've faded?
Who shows me horizons
where I once saw only walls?
Who embodies the principles I hold dear —
or the life I yearn for in silence?
What hard lessons, born of struggle,
revealed truths comfort could not?

Don't hold out for an ideal sage.
Guidance often hides in plain sight —
its presence humble,
its impact profound.
The teacher appears not in robes of wisdom,
but in the image of those who've walked before you,
leaving footprints where you feared no path existed.

Key Insight

Mentors don't hand you strength —
they reveal it was always yours.
Their gift isn't control.
It's clarity.
They hold up a mirror
when your vision of yourself blurs —
showing you your resilience,
your insight,
your readiness for more.
You don't take courage from a mentor.
You reclaim your own.

The Power of Community

Growth thrives in connection.
A mentor's spark can ignite your journey,
but a community's collective strength
keeps it burning.

Surround yourself with those
carving bold paths of their own,
and your courage deepens.
You feel less isolated.
You feel seen.

Seek spaces that fuel your transformation —
where truth is embraced,
where growth is voiced openly,
where others, too, reach for more.

A trusted accountability partner
who holds you to your truth.
A mastermind group
that both challenges and uplifts you.
A book circle, a workshop, a retreat
that widens your view.
An online haven of like-minded souls
reminding you: *you're not alone.*

A true community doesn't just push you —
it believes in you.
It carries your vision when your grip falters.
It reflects your potential
when you lose sight of your own strength.

The Mentor Within

Not all guidance flows from external voices.
Deep within you resides a subtler force —
your intuition,
your inner sage.

Often drowned by fear, distraction, or chaos,
this voice doesn't demand attention.
It bides its time,
waiting for you to create space,
to pause,
to listen with intent.

You can nurture this connection
by fostering what lets it rise.
Embrace solitude.
Write freely, unjudged.
Meditate.
Walk in nature, unplugged.
Heed your dreams.
Pose honest questions —
and let answers unfold without haste.

This inner mentor rarely speaks in clear prose.
It offers a nudge,
a spark of certainty,
a truth that resonates beyond words.
Its direction is unwavering.
Follow it, even in small steps,
and it will steer you true.

Guidance Isn't Always Comfortable

Your truest teachers
may not feel like mentors at first.
They might unsettle you,
prod you,
urge you to face inner demons
you've tucked away.

Growth doesn't bloom in ease.
It thrives at the boundary —
in the strain,
the tension,
the call to outgrow your former self.

Authentic mentorship —
even the unexpected kind —
demands you rise.

It might take the form of:
A book that upends your perspective.
A friend who delivers hard truths with care.
A coach or therapist who holds you to account.
A setback that forces you to pivot, adapt, and grow.

Not all guidance feels gentle.
Sometimes it arrives as disruption.
But even unease can teach —
if you embrace its lessons.

Action Step: Call In a Mentor

Choose one mentor to join you on this path.
They may be living, remembered, imagined,
or the steady voice within your core.

Reflect on their presence:
What wisdom do they offer?
What strengths do they reflect back to you?
What part of you do they inspire or fortify?

Now, welcome their wisdom into your journey.
Through their words in a book,
a direct conversation,
or simply holding their essence in your mind —
let their influence guide your next step.

Ask with honesty and courage:
If this mentor spoke to me now,
what would their message be?

Write it freely.
Listen deeply.
The truth that emerges may surprise you.

The Light of Guidance

Mentors don't erase the struggle.
They cast clarity on the road before you.
Their voice might reach you across a table,
through the lines of a weathered page,
or from the steady core of your own heart.

No matter their form,
their message is constant —
a truth your soul aches to reclaim:
You are never alone.

The hero you seek,
the strength you long for,
has always burned within you,
waiting for the moment you dare to claim it.
Step forward now, carrying their light,
and trust the path unfolding.

1.5 Crossing the Threshold: Embracing the Challenge

Every journey hinges on a single moment —
when indecision yields to action.
This is the *crossing of the threshold* —
the point where retreat is no longer an option.

The call has been answered.
The familiar world, with its comforts and limits,
fades behind you.
Ahead lies the uncharted —
boundless, daunting, alive with possibility.

In myth, the hero strides through the gate,
ventures into the wild,
steps into the tempest.
In life, it may be less dramatic —
yet no less profound.
It's the day you walk away from a role
that dims your fire.
The morning you forge a new path,
not because you feel prepared,
but because you refuse to wait any longer.
The instant you embrace what terrifies you —
yet sets your soul ablaze.
The night you voice a truth —
first to yourself,
then to another.

Crossing the threshold sparks true transformation.
It's not the end of fear —
but the choice to pursue growth despite it.

You linger at the edge,
not from weakness,
but because a part of you senses
there's no going back.
The threshold is a fleeting bridge —
no guardrails,
no markers,
only the rhythm of your own resolve
and a deep certainty:
This is real.

No perfect moment will arrive.
No absolute clarity will save you.
There's only the weight of staying small
against the pull of something greater.

This is the sacred tension —
fear meeting your becoming.
And in this pause,
this breath before the leap,
your transformation takes root.

Why This Stage Matters

This moment is more than a symbol —
it's hallowed ground.

It's the pivot from intention to action,
from envisioning change
to actually stepping into its reality.

Crossing the threshold is a silent oath —
not spoken,
but lived.
It's one thing to dream of a new life,
to scribble it in journals,
to voice it in fleeting moments or hushed confessions.
It's another to move toward it,
knowing the past will not hold its shape.

This stage divides wishing
from the action of becoming.

No promises await on the other side —
only the stark truth
that the life you seek
demands a new you to rise.

That rise begins with one unyielding step.
Not rooted in certainty,
but in devotion —
to the unknown,
to your growth,
to forging a self that carries
the shadow of who you were
into the light of who you'll be.

Commitment in Action

Crossing the threshold is an act —
a moment where your life mirrors
your deepest yearning.
You don't need the entire path laid bare.
You don't need to see the journey's end.

What matters is the courage
to take that first, deliberate step —
small, unsteady, or uncertain as it may be.

It might look like:
Enrolling in the course you've dodged time and again.
Writing that raw, unpolished first line.
Scheduling the therapy session you've long delayed.
Voicing your resolve aloud —
even if your words waver.

Each action becomes a vow.
A bold signal to existence —
I'm choosing growth.
I'm done with waiting.

Ask yourself:
What single action can I take today
to honor the change I've embraced?
What does crossing this threshold
look like for me — right now?

Then act.
Not because you're fully prepared —
but because each step shapes you
into someone ready.

The Courage to Let Go

Crossing the threshold is not just about
what you embrace —
it's about what you let go.
It means shedding the false comfort
of the old world —
the habits, roles, and selves
that once anchored you,
even as they confined your growth.

Even if unfulfilling,
the familiar holds a subtle power.
But true expansion demands release.
No growth blooms in stagnation.
To reshape your life,
you must dare to loosen your grip on who you were.

Letting go might mean:
Casting off outdated identities —
the caretaker, the overachiever,
the one who never seeks support.
Parting with bonds that no longer align
with your truth —
even if they once felt like home.

Releasing the burden of perfectionism
for the sake of motion,
progress,
becoming.

It's not always a grand gesture.
Sometimes letting go is as simple
as choosing a new thought,
a fresh stance,
a bolder way to inhabit your own life.

Each release of what no longer serves you,
carves space
for what is ready to take root.

Key Insight

Courage doesn't mean fear vanishes.
It's the decision to press forward,
not despite the fear —
but because a deeper force pulls you:
Your purpose.
Your truth.
Your unfolding self.
These outweigh the tremors of doubt —
they're why you keep going,
even with unsteady hands.
Fear becomes a companion, not a chain.
The shaking is proof you're alive,
reaching for something that matters.

Embracing the Unknown

Beyond the threshold stretches uncharted territory —
raw, untamed, laced with trials,
yet alive with discovery, wonder, and the truest you,
waiting to take shape.

Uncertainty is not your adversary.
It's the sacred ground
where transformation carves its mark.

The unknown will test you,
stretch you,
strip away what no longer fits.
But it will also refine you —
if you face it with an open heart,
if you let it create what must emerge.

Remember this:
No hero starts whole.
The journey molds them.
The fire tempers them.
And the unknown —
with all its shadows and brilliance —
is where you'll uncover parts of yourself
yet to be known.

Stepping into the unknown
is like moving through mist.
The full path hides from view.
Only the next step glimmers faintly.
The familiar recedes behind you,
and what lies ahead remains unshaped.

Yet mist carries its own strange grace.
It slows your pace,
sharpens your senses,
asks you to trust each step,
to feel more than hurry.

As you move forward,
the horizon widens —
not because the mist clears,
but because you've ventured deeper,
carrying your courage like a flame.

In time, you stop waiting for a clear road.
You walk —
because something within you knows:
This is the way.

Setting Your Intentions

Before you venture further,
pause.
This is your moment to claim what matters.

Not fixed plans,
not results carved in stone —
but intentions.
Guiding lights.
Values to carry close.
Truths to uphold,
no matter how the path turns and twists.

Intentions are your roots.
When the road grows rugged —
and it will —
they ground you in your purpose.

Ask yourself:
What change am I truly chasing?
What part of myself do I seek to rediscover or reveal?
What principles will I refuse to compromise
on this journey?
What will I no longer tolerate in my life?
What legacy am I building
with each choice I make today?

Write them clearly.
Speak them boldly.
Hold them as a lodestar
when doubt clouds your way.
Let these intentions steady your stride —
reminding you,
even in uncertainty,
of the course your heart has chosen.

Action Step: Declare Your Crossing

Choose one tangible act
to mark your commitment.
Something real.
Something now.
Enroll.
Attend.
Speak your truth.
Start what you've delayed.

You don't need to bound forward.
You don't need to feel fearless.
You only need to keep going.

Let this be your vow:
I've stepped beyond the known.
I'm here.
I'm becoming.

And today, that begins
with one honest step forward.

Journal Prompt:
What act — however small —
could stand as my bold claim to this crossing?
What does it mean, in my own heart, to say:
"I am no longer who I was"?
How can I anchor myself — when doubt creeps in —
to the truth that I've already started the journey?

The Choice That Ignites

Every transformation hinges on a single decision —
to release who you've been
and stride toward who you're destined to be.

That first step —
whether bold or faltering,
tentative yet undeniably yours —
marks the moment your true story begins.

You've crossed the boundary.
You've claimed your path.
But the journey doesn't soften
beyond the threshold —
it deepens,
unfolds into uncharted terrain.

Ahead lies the proving ground:
unforeseen trials,
unexpected allies,
buried fears drawn into sharp focus.

This is where your initiation truly takes root —
where the courage of your choice
meets the fire of what's next.

1.6 Tests, Allies, and Enemies: The First Initiation

Once you cross the threshold,
the journey begins to unfold — raw and unscripted.
The world beyond the familiar
isn't a peaceful meadow —
it's a crucible.

Here, your resolve is challenged.
Your commitment is tested.
Your hidden doubts rise to the surface.

You face obstacles that disregard your intentions,
relationships that reflect your unresolved wounds,
and resistance — both from within and without —
that probes relentlessly:
Are you truly in this?

This is your first initiation.
It's rough.
It's humbling.
It's hallowed.

In myth, this is where the hero meets trials,
finds companions,
encounters deceivers,
and learns to navigate an uncharted realm.
In life, it's less cinematic —
yet no less profound.

The thrill of beginning dulls,
and the work of becoming takes hold.
New habits falter.
Old fears resurface, cloaked in elaborate guises.
Doubt returns, armed with stronger arguments.

Yet alongside these —
glimmers of resilience you didn't know you possessed.
Brief bursts of clarity.
Unexpected support —
a friend's message, a line in a book,
a subtle inner shift.

This is where growth happens.
Real growth isn't polished or perfect.
It's true. It's hard-won.
And it belongs to you.

Why This Stage Matters

Crossing the threshold was a daring leap —
but holding the path
is where transformation truly takes hold.

Initiation doesn't demand a single burst of bravery.
It calls for many —
testing your endurance,
your resolve,
your choice to press on
when the initial thrill fades.

This stage matters because it separates
dreaming of change
from living it.
You're no longer sketching plans
or practicing in your mind.
You're immersed in the work —
navigating it,
stumbling through it,
evolving because of it.

This shift — from idea to reality —
is where the old you begins to unravel.
Transformation isn't born in the choice alone.
It grows in perseverance.

Tests and Trials:
The Universe Starts Asking Questions

Every transformation faces scrutiny.
It must.
The instant you declare: *I choose change*,
life responds with questions:

How far will you go?
How deeply are you in?
How true is your commitment?

Then the trials arrive.
Old patterns you thought you'd shed
resurface —

slipping through when you're weary,
exposed,
unguarded.

Those around you may challenge your shift,
question your new boundaries,
tug you back toward the self you've outgrown.
Your own resistance wears clever masks —
procrastination posing as rest,
perfectionism dressed as ambition,
overthinking veiled as planning.

Just as you find your balance,
life throws a curve:
an unforeseen hurdle
demanding sharper focus,
clearer intent,
and more of you.

These aren't punishments.
They're calls to deepen.
Markers on the path.

Each trial urges your confirmation,
to live the beliefs you claim,
to carve your new self through action.

Transformation isn't a single spark of insight —
it's built through repetition,
practice, one deliberate choice at a time.

Navigating Setbacks as Tests

Not every test arrives with fanfare.
Some creep in subtly,
masked as ordinary stumbles.
A missed chance.
A fading drive.
A flicker of doubt that murmurs:
Maybe this isn't meant to be.
A moment that feels like retreat,
pulling you to question all you've built.

You might feel drained,
restive, cut off from your own progress.
But these aren't signs of defeat.
They are turning points —
moments where growth reshapes itself.

The journey slows,
not to torture you,
but to call forth a deeper resolve.

Setbacks carve sharper questions:
Will you stand by yourself, even in struggle?
Will you keep going,
even when the way feels blurred?

Growth isn't gauged by speed —
it's forged in how you rise
when the ground seems to crumble beneath you.

Key Insight

Growth doesn't come from sidestepping challenges.
It comes from facing them —
with focus,
with intent,
and with the steady resolve to keep moving forward.

Allies: The Ones Who Walk Beside You

You're not meant to tread this path alone.
As the journey grows steeper,
allies emerge.
Some are lifelong companions.
Others are mentors, partners, or kind strangers
whose words land precisely when you need them.

They rekindle your resilience
when your own conviction falters.
They honor your small triumphs
and hold room for your doubts —
without judgment,
without rushing to mend you.

Reflect:
Who champions your growth
without steering its course?
Who sees a spark in you
you're still learning to trust?
Which bonds align with the path you're forging —
not just the one you've left behind?

If allies feel scarce, seek them out.
Join a circle.
Share your truth with someone worthy of it.
Surround yourself with voices
that challenge and elevate.
Engage with words that stretch your spirit,
and walk with those who know how to truly hear.

Allies don't always arrive on your schedule.
But when your heart opens —
when you're ready to receive —
they find their way to you.

Enemies and Shadows:
Recognizing Resistance in All Its Forms

Not every person —
nor every piece of you —
will champion your transformation.
The "enemies" you encounter
don't always brandish weapons,
yet they can hinder,
slowing your journey to who you're becoming.

They might appear as:
A companion who questions your path,
their doubts rooted in their own fear of change.
A space that saps your vitality,
muddling your focus with distraction or apathy.
The inner voice that insists you'll fall short —

that this dream is too vast for you.
Old patterns cloaked in familiarity,
luring you back to a smaller self.
Comparisons that whisper:
you're too late, lacking,
already outpaced.

These aren't villains to be destroyed.
They're patterns to discern.
The aim isn't to battle blindly —
but to see clearly,
to name,
to understand how resistance takes hold.

When you name it,
you claim authority over it.
Clarity, not constriction,
becomes your response.

Shadow Allies:
When Resistance Becomes a Teacher

Not every ally feels like a friend.
Sometimes, those who unsettle you,
provoke you,
question your path —
are sculpting you too.

The colleague who doubts your choices?
The conflict that demands your voice?

The hurdle that strains your patience,
your boundaries,
your will?
They may be honing your strength,
exposing your edges
so you can grow beyond them.

Shadow allies don't offer solace.
They bring refinement.
They don't pave an easier road —
they forge a truer one.

Meet them with clarity,
not resistance,
and they transform into unexpected mentors.
Not through warmth,
but by revealing the courage and truth
you've yet to fully embrace.

Action Step: Map the Landscape

Open your journal and create three columns:
Tests | Allies | Resistance

Now pause and reflect.
Since crossing the threshold:
What obstacles have risen to challenge you?
Who has stepped forward to bolster your journey —
directly or unexpectedly?

What forms of pushback — internal or external —
have made themselves known?

Be candid. Be open.
Let your thoughts spill without critique.

Patterns will surface.
Cycles will come into focus.
With this clarity,
you'll navigate the path with greater skill,
sharper awareness,
and deeper resolve.

Seeing the terrain clearly
is the first stride toward moving through it
with purpose.

Your First Initiation

This stage is the heart of your transformation —
not the flawless moment,
but the raw, human one.
The path is no longer a distant vision.
It's real,
lived in each breath,
each struggle,
each step toward becoming.

Struggle isn't failure.
It's evolution.

With every challenge met,
every ally embraced,
every shadow named —
you forge a new self,
carved by each deliberate choice.

You take the pain and the what-ifs,
and you weave them into a narrative
that propels you forward.
Keep moving.
Through the weight.
Through the ache.
Each step gets you closer to who you're meant to be.

Closing the Departure Phase: The First Steps Into Becoming

Every profound change begins not with movement,
but with a spark of awareness —
a fracture in the old narrative that insists:
This cannot be all there is.

And you heard it.
You traced the contours of your Ordinary World,
discerning what nourished you —
and what held you back.
You felt the call — faint or fierce —
and stood amid your fears,
grappling with whether you should answer.

Guidance found you in unlikely forms.
A strength within stirred,
long dormant, now rising to meet you.
And you chose to act.
That choice alone is a triumph.

The Departure phase is more than a beginning.
It's the shattering of a trance —
the one that bound you
to a life of familiar roles and routines.
It marks the end of drifting through existence
and the dawn of something greater, bolder,
more you.

This is where you took your first strides
toward becoming.
The path ahead will wind and challenge,
bringing trials,
doubts,
moments that test your core
and reshape who you believe you are.

But let this truth root deep:
You've already started.
You're no longer poised at the edge of the unknown.
You've crossed into it.

That step —
taken with unsteady hands
but an open heart —
plants the seed
for every transformation yet to unfold.

Key Insight

Transformation doesn't demand perfection.
It sparks the instant you act.
One step —
chosen with purpose,
fueled by heart —
is sacred.
It shatters old cycles.
It rewrites your narrative.
It declares: *I'm ready to begin my journey.*

Self-Reflection: Honor the Journey Thus Far

Before you press onward,
pause to glance back —
not with judgment,
but with reverence.

You've crossed a boundary many never near.
By choosing to act,
you've already shifted something important within.

Reflect:
What have you released —
in mind, heart, or body —
by stepping onto this path?
What have you uncovered about your resilience,
your doubts, your clarity
in these first strides?
And how do you face the road ahead —
not just its challenges,
but the potential it stirs within you?
What whispers of truth have grown
louder since you began?
What version of yourself
are you already leaving behind?

Let these questions settle.
Meet them with honesty.
The journey doesn't only stretch forward —
it deepens within.

Action Step: Declare Your Departure

Open your journal —
or simply pause and center yourself —
and voice these two truths aloud:

"I am leaving behind..."
(Name the patterns, roles, or convictions
that no longer fit the self you're shaping.)

"I am moving toward…"
(Claim the life, the growth, the purpose
that draws you forward.)

Speak deliberately.
Speak as if sealing a vow.
This is your commitment —
not only to the world,
but to your own heart.

A boundary has been crossed.
A new story has begun.
And you are the one who chose to write it.

Closing Thought

Every worthwhile journey is born in the unknown.
Not in answers,
but in the bravery to move forward without them.

You never needed guarantees —
only the resolve to embrace what lies ahead.
And you have.

You've drawn the first breath of a new narrative.
Now let the story unfold.
Let the path reveal itself.
And trust in the becoming that has already begun.

5

THE INITIATION — TRIALS, GROWTH, AND TRANSFORMATION

Here, transformation begins to carve its form.
If the Departure was the spark —
a fracture, a call, a daring step into the unknown —
the *Initiation* is the blaze.
It's the kiln.
Where old identities unravel,
illusions dissolve,
and a deeper truth starts to rise.
This is where your new self begins to emerge
and then to harden.

This stage doesn't feel heroic.
It breaks you open —
raw, disquieting, often solitary,
yet sacred in its insistence
that you meet yourself without pretense.

No crowds to cheer you on.
No clear milestones guide the way.
No signs confirm you're on course.
Only the quiet, inward work of becoming unfolds.

Here, the ego frays —
and the soul finds its voice.
Only then does the ascent begin.

Not because the path grows lighter,
but because something within you
stops craving ease
and starts claiming its own strength.

The Road of Trials: Where Growth Is Earned

Growth is never given.
It's earned —
shaped through each challenge, choice, and misstep.

In myth, the hero battles dragons,
navigates mazes,
faces deities demanding the impossible.
In life, the adversaries are quieter —
procrastination, doubt, perfectionism, exhaustion.
They don't bellow.
They linger,
sapping momentum with subtle persistence.

There's no detour around fear.
No shortcut to resilience.
No way to ponder your way through
what demands to be lived.

Here, the work becomes tangible —
and so does the change.
You may feel the urge to turn back.
You may question if this path is yours after all.

But these trials don't mark failure.
They signal you're immersed in the journey —
fully, deeply, truly.

If you stay and soldier on,
meeting each moment with honest presence,
however flawed,
you'll build something unbreakable.
Not a life without struggle —
but one alive with strength.

Support and Connection: Allies on the Path

No one navigates this phase in isolation —
nor should they.
Support finds you,
often from unexpected corners.

A friend's steady words,
arriving just as you teeter on surrender.
A book that doesn't merely resonate —
it stirs something dormant,
igniting a spark you didn't know you carried.
A community, a gathering,
or even a fleeting exchange
that echoes one truth:
You are not alone.

These allies don't bear your burden.
They don't tread your path.
But they bring presence,
clarity,
and warmth
when your own resolve wavers.

They are mirrors,
reflecting your bravery
when you've lost sight of it.
They are roots,
not to bind you,
but to ground you
when the storm pulls you to retreat.

In a world that prizes solitary strength,
these moments of connection remind you:
We were never meant to journey alone.

Sometimes, the boldest act
is to accept support —
not out of weakness,
but from the courage to release pride.

Temptation and Distraction: The Lure Off the Path

As you delve deeper into the journey,
temptation doesn't vanish —
it evolves.
It grows subtler,
sharper,
harder to pin down.

It doesn't always wear the mask of sabotage.
Sometimes it cloaks itself in busyness,
overcrowded schedules,
a quick scroll online
that stretches into lost time,
or a sudden task that distracts your focus
before you take your next brave step.

It tries to seduce in surrender:
Just take a break.
You've done enough.
Maybe this isn't the right time after all.

Perhaps it's the invitation
to binge-watch instead of write,
or the sudden urge to reorganize your entire house
when you should be making that difficult phone call.

But these aren't moments of necessary rest.
They're diversions —
fleeting comforts that nudge you off track.

The challenge is quiet but real:
Stay present.
Hold fast to your purpose
when distraction feels like ease.
Recognize that comfort, untethered to meaning,
can become a subtle trap.

Discipline, awareness, and focus
are your guides.
Not rigid rules —
but reminders of what matters most
when the world pulls you to forget.

Atonement and Revelation: The Deep Inner Reckoning

Every important journey turns inward in time.
The external challenges yield to a deeper truth —
one far more daunting.

This is the reckoning.
The unveiling.
The moment when the masks slip,
and you confront the depths you've long avoided.

Here, you meet your shadow —
the buried beliefs,
the inherited scars,
the warped identities that have silently shaped you.
You see the roles you've played,
the narratives you've carried,
the pieces of yourself you've forsaken to fit in.

Slowly, with raw honesty, truth rises.
Not just about the world —
but about you.

This isn't a collapse.
It's a return.
You cease fleeing your pain.
You stop bargaining with your values.
And you begin the sacred act of reclaiming.

Not by crafting a new self —
but by rediscovering who you were
before the world told you to be someone else.
By embracing all that you are —
imperfect, luminous, unfinished, true.

The Boon: Claiming the Gift of the Journey

Every challenge bears a gift.
It might be clarity, strength, insight,
or a hard-won calm.
Or perhaps it's the simple, profound knowing
that you met the trial —
and emerged transformed.

This is the *boon*:
the treasure forged through grit, presence,
and resolve.
It may not match what you sought.
But it's precisely what your soul needed.

Yet the journey doesn't end here.
The Initiation is a midpoint, not a finish line.
It's the flame that hones your courage,
the descent that paves the way for your rising.

All you've endured has prepared you
for what comes next.
You now hold something rare —
not flawless character,
but wisdom earned.

With that wisdom comes a new call:
To return.
To weave what you've gained into your life.
To embody what you've learned.

That is the road forward.
Are you ready to walk it?

You've braved the fire.
You've met yourself with raw honesty.
Now, true integration begins —
not as an idea, but as lived truth.

In the steps ahead, we'll tread that path together.

2.1 The Road of Trials: Building Strength Through Adversity

Transformation doesn't begin with victory.
It begins with a plunge —
into the depths of challenge, unease, and uncertainty.

In myth, this is the *Belly of the Whale* —
where the hero is engulfed,
severed from the familiar world.
It's disorienting.
It's raw.
It's humbling.
Yet — it's sacred.

Because here, amid struggle and stillness,
something vital takes root.

The modern journey holds no mythical creatures
or enchanted caverns,
but the weight is no less profound.
You step into a space where the old self frays —
and the new self,
not yet fully formed,
begins to emerge.

The ground trembles.
The air shifts.
This is no longer a theory.
It's real.
The discomfort is real.
The trials are real.

And you are called to rise in ways
you've never dared before.

Understanding the Challenge

What is your "whale"?
What is the first obstacle
demanding more than mere intent —
calling for your full, unyielding presence?

The Road of Trials takes many forms:
A rejection after a daring leap.
A misstep that rattles your belief in yourself.
A health crisis, a financial blow,
an emotional fracture you didn't see coming.
Old scars resurfacing,
ones you thought long healed.

This might look like the promotion
you thought you wanted
leaving you feeling empty,
or the relationship you fought to save
teaching you that some things must end
for new life to begin.

Sometimes the test is external —
a disruption that throws you off balance.
Other times, it wells up from within —
a subtle doubt that creeps in:
You're not ready.
You're not enough.
Turn back now.

But every challenge carries its purpose.
Not to wound you.
Not to shatter you.
But to stir you awake.
To reveal the strength still dormant within.
To test the depth of your will to grow.

The road doesn't ask who you dream of being.
It demands to know who you'll forge yourself into —
here, in the heat of the moment.

Surrendering to the Process

You cannot force transformation through sheer will.
At this stage, progress may not dazzle onlookers.
It may look like a pause.
Reflection.
A quiet unraveling.

It may call you to shed what no longer belongs —
old roles, worn-out habits,
the heavy shield of perfectionism
you've carried too long.

Surrender isn't defeat.
It's clearing ground.
It's the sacred courage
to be molded by a force greater than fear.

It's the bold release of who you've been,
making way for the self
you were always destined to become.

Learning from Failure

We're taught to dread failure —
to view it as evidence of our inadequacy.

But on the hero's path,
failure isn't the end.
It's the crucible.

It uncovers truths comfort hides.
It humbles pride.
Hones clarity.
Builds resilience.

It asks:
Will you rise again — not once, but repeatedly —
each time wiser, bolder, more complete?

Every misstep carries a lesson.
Every stumble, a chance to learn.
You don't fail by falling.
You fail only by staying down.

Reflect:
What did this teach me?
What strength did I find?
What fear lost its grip
when I refused to quit?
What part of me emerged
that I didn't know existed?
What will I do differently now?

Each honest answer
fortifies your resolve —
adding another line
to the story of who you're becoming.

Tests, Allies, and Enemies

As you immerse yourself in the journey,
the terrain transforms.
You begin to discern what walks with you —
and what subtly holds you back.

Tests take countless shapes:
Old habits resurfacing,
stubbornly clinging despite your growth.
New demands pressing harder than you expected.
Sudden setbacks that unsettle your balance.
These aren't roadblocks —
they're calls to renew your resolve.

Allies emerge as people, practices,
or glimpses of the self you're becoming —
an inner voice urging:
Press on.
They mirror your resilience
when it feels out of reach.
They hold your truth steady
when doubt begins to creep.
They stand with you in the unseen struggles,
where the weight of the work is yours alone.

Enemies aren't always outside you.
They may be the sting of comparison,
the pull of familiar ruts,
the quiet erosion of self-doubt or cynicism.
Or they may be those unsettled by your change,
wishing you'd remain as you were.

And sometimes —
the enemy becomes your sharpest teacher.
Not because they're correct in their message,
but because they expose
what in you still seeks healing.

Key Insight

Growth doesn't come from dodging challenges.
It comes from facing them —
with focus and intent.
Each trial tests not your perfection,
but your persistence.
You're not being punished.
You're being forged —
for resilience,
for clarity,
for the self this path is summoning.

Action Step: Take Inventory of Your Journey So Far

In your journal, pause and reflect:
What challenge confronts you now?

What does it call you to fortify, let go, or embrace?
Who or what has bolstered your path thus far?
Name your allies — even the subtle ones.
What resistance has surfaced — within or without?
What habits, beliefs, or roles must you reshape
or let go
to step forward unburdened?

Charting your inner and outer terrain fosters clarity.
And clarity fuels the courage to continue.

The Unbinding

This is not the end.
It's a crossing.
Here —
deep in the core of your transformation —
you are not unraveling.
You are being reformed.

This descent mirrors ancient tales —
what mystics named the *underworld*.
Not a place of torment,
but of reckoning.
Like Dante stepping into the Inferno,
or Neo breaking free from the Matrix,
you must release the illusions
that once cloaked you in comfort
but now obscure your truth.

This is not yet arrival.
It's liberation.
Not the crafting of a new self,
but the shedding of who you never truly were.

What you uncover here —
your fears, your strength, your essence —
forms the foundation
of what you're going to build next.

Keep moving.
Something vital is taking form within you.
The road continues,
and you are ready for what it will ask.

2.2 The Road of Trials: The Crucible of Becoming

Beyond the threshold,
the familiar falls away —
yet no clear path unfolds.
This is the proving ground.

Here, your remaking isn't merely envisioned —
it's carved through effort.
Progress twists, stumbles, deepens,
loops back on itself.
One trial yields to the next.
Each lesson builds the foundation for what follows.

Through friction, fire, and failure,
a new self begins to emerge.
This isn't punishment.
It's preparation.

Every challenge sheds what no longer fits.
Every falter forges a stronger core.
This is how your soul reclaims its resilience —
not in a single leap,
but trial by trial.

Confronting the Challenges

On the Road of Trials,
the terrain is rugged —
within and without.

You may encounter:
Rejection that rattles your confidence.
Setbacks that demand to rethink your approach.
Self-doubt that clouds your vision.
Resistance from others who fear your growth.
Weariness of the heart
as buried wounds surface,
insisting on being acknowledged.

These aren't signs you've lost your way.
They're proof you're on a path that counts.

Each challenge carries a subtle question:
Are you ready to grow beyond the self you've known?

Key Insight
    Trials are not punishments —
    they are turning points.
    Each one offers a sacred call:
    Will you embrace the next step of your growth —
    not with certainty,
    but with bold resolve?

Cultivating Resilience

To press onward,
resilience becomes your foundation.
Not the armor of future perfect self —
but a steady, enduring strength
to stumble, pause, recalibrate,
and rise anew.

Reflect:
What patterns do these trials uncover?
What strengths are taking shape in this forge?
What truths have I avoided — or resisted?

Self-compassion and clear-eyed honesty
are your steadfast allies here.
You don't need to be flawless.
You don't need all the answers.
You only need to keep showing up.

Building New Capacities

Each trial is an initiation —
a call to forge new strengths,
both within and in practice.

You may be called to:
Craft stronger routines.
Bolster your emotional stamina.
Reframe entrenched beliefs.
Learn to say *No* — with clarity, without apology.
Embrace new habits, roles, or identities.

This isn't transient change.
It's a deep reweaving of your core beliefs.

True growth doesn't skirt struggle —
it rises from it.
What you build here
is the inner framework
to carry forward.

Action Step: Reframe the Struggle

Select one challenge you're facing now.
Turn toward it fully —
not with judgment,
but with curiosity.

Write it at the top of a page.
Below, list three specific ways
this challenge has already changed you —
even in small ways.

Ask yourself:
What lesson is this moment offering me?
How is it calling me to evolve?
What mindset, practice, or resource can carry me forward?

Write your thoughts.
Linger with them.
Let clarity surface, even in pieces —
and honor what comes.

This isn't about forcing answers.
It's about seeing the struggle
as a vital part of your ascent.

Then identify one concrete action
you can take this week
to lean into the growth it's offering.

Forged in the Fire

You're not merely surviving this stage —
you're being sculpted by it.
This is the crucible of transformation.
Not a retribution —
but a refining flame.

Every setback sharpens your will.
Every effort carves a stronger core.
Every tear hones your spirit
into something tougher,
truer.

What emerges isn't just a stronger you —
but a self closer to your essence,
stripped of what no longer aligns.

Keep moving forward.
The next challenge may loom,
but so does the next version of you —
bolder, clearer, more whole,
ready to meet what lies ahead.

2.3 Meeting the Goddess: Finding Allies and Support

There comes a moment on the journey
when the weight of struggle makes you pause —
not to ponder answers or solutions,
but to take in what may yet to come.

A steady force steps into your path.
Not to mend. Not to rescue. But to walk alongside.
And something within the hero softens.
For even the boldest cannot tread alone forever.
Transformation, though deeply yours,
was never meant to be a solitary act.

In myth, this is when the *Goddess* emerges:
a symbol of wisdom, compassion, and clarity.
She may appear as a mentor, a companion,
a memory,
or a spark of the divine within you.
She doesn't lift you through the flames —
she reminds you that you're not consumed by them.

She offers no shortcuts, no escapes.
Only presence.
Only truth.
Only a voice that echoes:
You don't have to travel alone.

This is the turning point
where the hero begins to see:
Support is not a sign of weakness.
It's woven into the journey's fabric.
A vital force that mirrors
what we often lose sight of —
our worth, our potential,
our connection to something greater.

In embracing that reflection,
something timeless and potent stirs awake.

Embracing Connection

In myth, this is the *Meeting with the Goddess* —
a sacred encounter with healing, wisdom, and grace.

She embodies compassion.
Intuition.
The quiet truth that your feelings hold weight,
and you, as you are, are enough.

In life, this presence takes countless forms:
A conversation that stirs something profound within.
A community that mirrors your growth
when your own vision falters.
A book, a quote,
a quiet moment of stillness
that calls you back to your own truth.

Sometimes, it's not another soul.
It's an inner alignment —
a deep release,
a voice rising from within.

These moments don't arrive with grandeur.
They come gently —
yet strike with force.
And when they do,
something guarded in you begins to yield.
Begins to open and say:

Yes to trusting.
Yes to receiving.
Yes to being met,
exactly as you stand.

Even one true connection can reshape your path.
For sometimes, what transforms you most
isn't guidance,
or striving
or strategy and plans —
but being truly seen.

The Strength to Be Seen

To embrace this support,
you must dare to be seen.
Vulnerability becomes the bridge.

This isn't the armored hero charging forward.
It's the seeker who pauses to admit,
I need help.

Vulnerability doesn't diminish your strength.
It makes you human.
It shows that true power
lies not in bearing every burden alone —
but in knowing when to share the load.

To allow another to walk beside you.
To let yourself be held —
not out of fragility,
but because you are worthy of care.

Healing doesn't always demand more effort.
Sometimes, it simply flows from being met —
fully,
gently,
without needing to prove your worth.

Recognizing the Support Around You

Allies wear many faces.
A mentor or coach
who challenges you to grow.
A friend who trusts in your potential
when your own faith wavers.
A partner who holds space for your evolution
without needing to rush it.
A book, a podcast, a ritual
that untangles inner chaos
and calls you back to your truth.

These goddess moments
may arrive as gentle affirmation —
or as a jolt that shakes you awake.
Their message remains constant:
You are not alone.

Often, it's this truth —
not a solution,
not a cure for all ills —
that shifts the entire journey.

Reflection Prompt

Who in your life nurtures your growth —
not for the self they wish you to be,
but for the truth of who you are?
Who holds faith in you
when your own belief falters?
Who offers honest words —
not to judge,
but to spark your becoming?

The Power of Supportive Relationships

True support isn't mere a nod of approval —
it can be a resonance of kindred spirits.
Not just a cheer from the sidelines,
but a presence that recalls your essence
when you've lost sight of it.

Strong bonds do more than soothe —
they stretch you.
They anchor you
through the tides of emotion.
They bring clarity
when doubt obscures your path.
They hold room for you
when fear or weariness urges retreat.
They summon you back
to your deepest truths
when the way grows dim.

This kind of support doesn't merely lift —
it ignites.
Not by carrying your weight,
but by walking with you
until you accept
you were never meant to bear it all alone.

Receiving As a Practice

Allowing others to stand with you
may feel foreign —
even unsettling.
But receiving is a craft of the heart.

It softens your edges.
It fortifies your spirit.
It reveals that growth isn't about striving harder —
but about being more present,
more open,
more true.

You don't need perfection to deserve support.
You need only willingness to receive.

In time, you may find:
the support you once longed for
becomes the support you're ready to give.

Not because you've mastered everything —
but because you've learned
to remain open
in the embrace of shared care.

Key Insight

You were never meant to transform alone.
True strength doesn't shine in solitude —
it grows through connection.
Embracing support
is not a sidestep from your journey.
It is the journey.

Action Step: Open the Door to Connection

Reach out to someone who lifts your spirit —
a friend, a mentor, a guide,
or a community that's quietly called to you.

Share where you stand.
Offer something true.
Welcome connection into your path.

You don't need the perfect words.
You need only the courage to extend your hand.

Sometimes, the boldest act is to say:
I'm still finding my way.
But I'm moving forward.
Will you walk with me?

The Power of Being Met

There is courage in standing alone —
but there is alchemy in being truly seen.
You were not meant to bear this journey in isolation.
Not because you lack strength,
but because you are human.

Support is not the opposite of strength —
it deepens it,
sustains it,
gives it room to flourish.
It transforms solitary endurance
into shared becoming.

Dare to be seen.
Allow yourself to be held.
And in time,
become a beacon for others
still discovering their path.

Your journey is yours to tread —
but it was always meant
to be walked with love.

This road now turns toward integration,
where the lessons you've gathered
begin to weave into the fabric of your life.

2.4 Temptation and Distraction: The Lure to Quit

Every pivotal journey harbors a moment —
often subtle, sometimes crushing —
when the path stretches endless,
and the promise of transformation dims into haze.

You've traveled far.
You're weary.
And in the quiet corners,
a voice begins to beckon:
Turn back.
You've done enough.
Comfort awaits here.
No one will judge you for pausing.
Perhaps this was never meant to be.

This is temptation's call.
Not the loud lure of vice or total collapse,
but a quieter pull.

It cloaks itself in reason,
drapes itself in logic,
whispers of one more day's rest.

It doesn't demand.
It persuades.
It frames comfort as wisdom,
the dream as too vast, too daring, too late —

retreat as the sensible choice,
the safe return
to the self you've outgrown.

The danger lies in its timing —
striking not when you're frail,
but when you've poured out more
than you knew you held.
It speaks in your voice,
making surrender sound like care.

But even as you grow stronger,
even as allies appear,
the journey presents its strongest challenge yet...

The Many Faces of Temptation

In myth, the *Temptress* lures the hero astray —
a figure weaving enchantment to derail the quest.
In your journey,
temptation takes subtler forms.

It might appear as a sensible excuse,
crafted with flawless logic.
An old habit,
fitting you like a worn glove.
A gleaming distraction,
masquerading as a golden chance.
A limiting belief,
dressed as a grounded reason.

Sometimes, temptation mimics progress —
posing as productivity,
feeling like love,
calling itself busyness
or even self-care.

But anything that draws you away
from your deeper purpose —
no matter how gentle,
how rational,
how familiar —
is a detour in disguise.

Recognizing the Voices of Temptation

Temptation rarely shouts.
It murmurs, swirled in familiar,
persuasive tones —
mimicking wisdom,
slipping past your guard.

It might say:
You've done enough. Take a rest.
This isn't working. Maybe it's time to shift.
You're not enough to see this through.
Perhaps this dream was never yours.

Or it creeps in more subtly —
procrastination veiled as planning,
overcrowded days dodging what truly counts,

self-sabotage hiding in the pursuit of perfection,
burnout dressed as a calculated retreat.

It's not always obvious.
But the more you attune to its cadence,
the less it can deceive you with its mask.

Key Insight
Temptation doesn't arise from weakness.
It surfaces because you stand at the brink
of something vital.
It's not failure — it's weariness.
Not fear — but the strain of growth.
The risk isn't in craving rest.
The risk is in confusing rest with retreat.

The Danger of Distraction

Distraction isn't merely lost time —
it's the cause of a fractured sense of self.
Each detour toward something easier
weaves a subtle narrative:
This dream isn't worth the struggle.

Repeat that tale often enough,
and it solidifies into conviction.
And convictions shape your reality.

Temptation doesn't always urge you
to abandon your path.
Sometimes, it nudges you to drift —
to stay busy, yet unmoored,
active, yet misaligned.

It might look like:
Falling back into old roles
because they're less daunting than moving forward.
Endlessly consuming content
instead of crafting something that matters.
Pursuing new aims
to sidestep the one that truly calls you.

These choices seem small.
But over time, they erode your focus —
sapping your resolve
bit by bit.

The Turning Point

This moment —
this pull to retreat —
is not defeat.
It's a threshold.
A sacred test.
A pause where your deeper self
calls for something more.

What do you truly seek —
ease or transformation?
Relief or purpose?
A life that's safe —
or one that's truly yours?

This crossroads arrives unannounced.
No trumpets, no signals mark its presence.
It may wear the guise of exhaustion,
doubt,
or another day where surrender seems simpler
than pressing on.

But here's the hidden truth:
Turning points rarely feel like pivots.
They feel like breaking points —
like *nothing is working*,
like *you fall short*,
like *it shouldn't be this hard*.

And that's why they matter.
What you choose next
reveals who you're becoming.

There's no shame in the struggle.
No fault in the faltering.
This isn't about certainty.
It's about conviction.

You could take the detour.
You could postpone your truth.
Or —
with one breath,
one step,
one line scrawled in your journal,
you can declare:
I will not forsake myself here.

The turning point
isn't shaped by how you feel.
It's defined by what you choose.

Reclaiming Focus and Staying Aligned

When temptation beckons,
don't chase force to resist.
Seek clarity.
Return to your *why*.
Voice it.
Write it.
Breathe it back into your body
like oxygen.

Ask:
Why did I set out on this path?
What vision would I forsake by turning back?
What part of myself do I guard — and honor —
by pressing forward?
Who could I become if I persist, even through struggle?

Nothing enduring is forged without resistance.
Resistance isn't a pointless barrier —
it's a sign you're nearing something crucial.

Lean on reflection.
Embrace ritual.
Renew your commitment.
Ground yourself again —
and again —
and again.

Action Step: Your Anti-Temptation Toolkit

Begin by identifying your three greatest temptations.
What pulls you off course most often?
Where does your momentum falter, and why?

Next, craft your responses.
What will you turn to in those moments?
A walk to clear your mind?
A moment to write your thoughts?
A message to someone who understands?

Then, set your anchors.
Place reminders in your world —
a quote on your mirror,
a photo on your desk,
a small token that roots you
in the truth of why you started this journey.

Your discipline needn't be bold or reckless.
It must simply be steadfast —
to your path,
to your purpose,
to the self that refuses to turn back.

Part of Your Path

Temptation isn't a sidetrack.
It's woven into your journey.
The hero isn't shaped by ease —
but by the choice to endure.

You don't rise despite this moment.
You rise because of it.

So pause, if you must.
Draw a steady breath.
Mend your spirit.
Tend to your wounds.
Restore the inner fire.
But don't mistake this moment
for the end.

You're not adrift.
You're in the thick of transformation.
And its fire —
fierce, relentless, refining —
is forging the next version of you.

The road ahead will demand more,
but it will also reveal
the strength you're building now.
Keep going.
Your journey is far from over.

2.5 Atonement and Revelation: Confronting Your Inner Shadows

Every outward journey leads inward in time.
After trials have worn down your armor,
after temptations have probed your resolve,
after distractions have lost their pull —
you face the truest challenge:
Yourself.

This is the reckoning.
A mirror without distortion.
A confrontation you can no longer avoid.

Joseph Campbell named this phase
the *Atonement with the Father* —
a mythic clash with what holds the hero back:
judgment, fear, towering authority.

In life, that force is often within.
An old self-image. A buried conviction.
A scar so familiar
it's woven into who you think you are.

This is no fight against the world.
It's a descent into the depths of your being —
a silent, essential encounter
with the shadows that still steer your path.

This is where healing begins.
But only if you dare to see
what's been hiding in plain sight.

Facing the Shadow Self

We all carry a shadow —
the repository of what we've learned to conceal:
shame, guilt, doubt, unhealed grief, insecurity.
Not because these are embarrassing flaws,
but because, long ago,
they were deemed unworthy to share.

So we buried them.
But buried is not vanished.

The shadow lingers, unseen —
steering your choices,
stoking your fears,
eroding your confidence
in ways that slip past notice.

Your shadow might whisper through:
The harsh inner critic
that drowns out encouragement.

Perfectionism that masks deep fear
of being seen as flawed.
People-pleasing that sacrifices your truth
for others' comfort.
Imposter syndrome
that convinces you your success is undeserved.

Rage that erupts when boundaries are crossed.
Or the inability to feel or express anger at all —
having learned long ago that expressing your fury
was "unacceptable" by societal or cultural norms.

The persistent belief that you must earn love
through achievement.
Or perhaps the opposite —
self-sabotage that destroys what you've built
before others can reject it first.

These aren't character flaws.
They're survival strategies that once served you
but now constrain the person you're becoming.

Ignoring them tightens their grip.
Denying their existence
grants them greater sway in defining
who you are.

Transformation ignites when you cease fleeing.
When you turn inward
and meet what you've dreaded.

Not to battle it —
but to see and name it clearly.

This might mean:
Voicing a past pain
you've never dared name aloud.
Uncovering actions
that stubbornly clash with your values.
Challenging beliefs
you inherited but never chose.

This work isn't easy.
It's not meant to be.
But it's the gateway to wholeness —
the moment where shame begins to unravel,
and truth starts to surface.

If this feels too heavy,
if the weight of what you discover
threatens to pull you under—
Pause.
Breathe.
You don't need to excavate everything at once.

Shadow work is not a race.
It's not about reaching for perfect conclusions
or complete healing.
It's about gentle, persistent curiosity
toward the parts of yourself you've kept hidden.

Start small.
Choose one pattern, one belief,
one recurring struggle.
Sit with it like you would as a frightened child —
with patience, not judgment.
With curiosity, not condemnation.

And remember:
You survived whatever created these shadows.
You have the strength to face them now —
not to destroy them,
but to understand them.

Reflection Prompt

What part of you have you pushed away —
concealed, dismissed, or muted?
Are there scars you've yet to fully confront,
still subtly guiding your steps in the world?
What truth have you hesitated to voice —
even in the quiet of your own soul?

Linger with these questions.
Not to condemn yourself —
but to start reclaiming
what you've left in the dark.

Yet seeing the shadow is only the first step.
The deeper work — the one that truly liberates —
asks you to extend mercy to what you discover there.

Different souls approach this work differently.
Honor your way:
If you're analytical by nature,
journal your observations.
Map the patterns.
Trace the threads back to their origins
with the precision of a researcher.

If you're more intuitive,
let the shadows speak through art, movement,
or dreams.
Dance with them.
Paint them.
Let them surface in whatever form feels true.

If you're action-oriented,
notice how these patterns play out in your daily life.
Catch yourself in the moment.
Choose differently, however small the choice.

If you're collaborative,
share this exploration with a trusted friend,
therapist, or guide.
Let another's presence hold space
for what feels too daunting to face alone.

There is no single right path through the shadows.
There is only your path —
the one that honors both your courage
and your limits.

The Power of Self-Forgiveness

Our resistance often stems
not from fear of failing —
but from guilt.
Guilt over past mistakes.
Guilt for not doing more.
Guilt for simply being human.

We convince ourselves that self-blame fuels growth,
that suffering makes us worthy.
But guilt doesn't promote change —
it stifles it.

Forgiveness isn't denial.
It's not forgetting.
Nor is it absolution.
It's seeing clearly —
acknowledging for what it was
and choosing to release.

By declaring:
Yes, I see what happened.
And I will not let it define me anymore.

It's not about ignoring the pain.
It's about refusing to let pain become who you are.
It's about taking the pain and the what-ifs,
and weaving them into a narrative
that propels you forward.

Ask yourself gently:
What have I been quietly punishing myself for?
What might it feel like to finally lay that burden down?
Who might I become if I stopped defining myself
by what I wish I'd done differently?

These questions demand more
than intellectual honesty.
They call for a different kind of courage entirely.

Key Insight

    Healing doesn't come from wiping away the past —
    it comes from choosing a new way to meet it.
    Transformation begins when you stop battling
    who you were
    and start nurturing who you're becoming.

Embracing Vulnerability

This stage demands a distinct courage —
not an armor, but a vulnerable heart.
Not a mask, but a raw presence.

You may need to face what you once buried.
To confess what you don't yet understand.
To seek support,
even if your words tremble.

This is true bravery —
born not in victory,
but through pain and tears.

You might be called to:
Voice a truth you've long avoided.
Dismantle inherited patterns
or break generational silence.

Let yourself fully feel
the weight of grief,
the sting of fear,
or the ache of longing.

You are not weak for struggling.
You are brave for staying present.
Brave for feeling deeply.
Brave for letting your heart stay open
in the presence of pain.

Redefining Power and Authority

This reckoning often stems
from internalized voices of authority —
parents, teachers, faith, culture —
each dictating who you should be.
You may still seek their validation,
shrink from their judgment,
or live by rules
that never belonged to you.

This is the deeper essence of atonement —
not just facing external forces,
but untangling the inner critic
they etched within you.
It's the moment you see
you've been scripted by another's story —
and now choose to author your own.

Ask yourself:
Who taught me what to fear?
Whose voice still echoes in my mind —
and do I still need to obey it?
What would it mean to define success, identity, and worth
on my own terms — starting now?

The Shift: From Shame to Sovereignty

No singular path winds through this inner terrain.

For some, it's ink poured onto journal pages,
raw thoughts spilling free.
For others, it's the quiet of therapy,
the solitude of reflection,
or a single, unguarded conversation
where truth finds its voice.

Yet the turning point
and what comes next is universal:
Shame begins to dissolve,
softening into self-acceptance.

Fear retreats,
giving way to a clearer, fiercer truth.
Pain, once a heavy chain,
reveals its hidden purpose —
a guide, not a captor.

This is the crux of transformation —
where your story ceases to be a wound,
a mark of what broke you,
and becomes instead a source of clarity,
a wellspring of hard-earned wisdom.

You claim the pen.
You write with a voice that's yours alone —
unshackled from old scripts,
unbound by others' expectations.

The page turns.
And with it,
you step into a sovereignty
that was always waiting to be claimed.

Action Step: The Inner Reckoning

1. Name the Shadow
Pinpoint the belief, habit, or voice
that holds you back,
keeping you tethered to a smaller self.

Write it clearly, unflinchingly.
Let it step into the light.

2. Uncover Its Roots
Where did this shadow take hold?
Whose words echo within it?
Was it learned, passed down, or absorbed?
Trace its origins to loosen its grip.

3. Reframe the Narrative
What truth will guide you now?
Turn the wound into a story of strength:
From: *I'm not enough.*
To: *I am evolving, worthy, and whole.*
Speak this new truth as a pledge,
firm and deliberate.

4. Release with Intention
Let go of the old story through action.
Burn the words that bound you.
Bury them in the earth.
Proclaim your new narrative under open skies.
Light a candle to mark the shift.
Write a letter to seal the change.
Create a symbol to anchor this moment.

This is how you close the chapter
without closing your heart.
This is how you begin anew —
on your own terms.

Reclaiming Your Freedom

You are not your past.
You are not the burdens
you bore to endure.
This stage was never about finding all answers —
it was about liberation.

You were never meant
to carry this weight endlessly.
Release it.
Reclaim your voice.
Reclaim your truth.

Step back into your life —
not as the one shaped by wounds,
but as the one who chooses now
to walk with clarity,
with compassion,
with intention.

You've faced the flames.
You didn't flinch.
You stayed.

Now, the next chapter is yours to shape.
The path ahead calls for your courage,
your hard-won wisdom,
your reclaimed power.

Move forward —
free, whole, and ready for what awaits.

2.6 The Revelation: Achieving Inner Transformation

True transformation hinges on a pivotal moment —
a quiet spark of insight
that pierces through doubt and uncertainty.

After weathering the descent into shadow,
enduring relentless trials,
and confronting your hidden truths,
a stillness settles.
A shift occurs.
A clarity arrives — not imposing, but undeniable.

In the Hero's Journey, this is *Apotheosis* —
a mythic ascent to the divine.
In your life, it feels earthier,
more human.
It's the instant you rise above your old narrative,
seeing its threads with a fresh perspective.

The fragments of your journey begin to align.
Not because the world has changed —
but because you have.

This isn't a victory seized by force.
It's won through release or even surrender,
through reflection,
through weaving your lessons into your being.

The old self softens, fades.
Masks slip away.
The noise quiets.

In their place rises something true and unmistakable:
Alignment of all the parts that produce
your new, blooming authentic self.
Now you don't merely grasp your path —
you feel its pulse in your bones.

This shift doesn't announce itself as a tremor.
It settles into your being like morning light —
gradual, then unmistakable.

A New Vision of Self

You are not the person who began this journey.
You've persevered.
You've questioned.
You've reached beyond the boundaries
of who you once believed you could be.

And now — something quiet, yet undeniable,
begins to take shape.
Not mere survival, but sovereignty.

You no longer brace against the world.
You move from your center —
with calm resolve, not haste.
With clarity, not desperation.

This isn't a moment of pomp.
It may not dazzle onlookers.
It may feel like coming home to yourself.
Like waking without fear, keeping your head up high.
Like choosing without betraying your values.
Like saying *no* without guilt
or claiming your truth —
perhaps silently,
but unflinchingly,
in the reflection of your own heart.

This is where *integration* begins.
Where understanding and insight
become a lived experience.
Where the path no longer feels like a chase —
and becomes a road unfolding
beneath your steady steps.

Signs of Apotheosis in Everyday Life

This phase of the journey
doesn't burst forth with grandeur.
It doesn't demand attention.
It arrives seamlessly,
settling into your day-to-day life.

You may notice:

A sense of inner peace
where chaos once reigned.
A subtle shift,
as a long-held belief
no longer aligns with the self you now claim.
A confidence that stands firm,
untethered from others' gaze or approval.
A sudden wellspring of compassion —
for yourself,
or even for someone who you once resented.

And then perhaps,
the deepest realization of all:
The journey itself
has been the actual transformation.
The catalyst of your becoming.

These signs are not loud.
They're modest,
found in the pause between breaths,
in the ease of a choice
made without second-guessing,
in the way you meet each new challenge
with steadiness you didn't know you held.

This is apotheosis —
not a crown of divinity,
but a consistent reclaiming of your own truth,
lived out in the ordinary moments
that may now feel extraordinary.

Reflection Prompt

What quiet truth has surfaced
from the depths of your trials?
What identities, beliefs, or roles
are you ready to set free?
And how might it feel —
in your body, your choices, your relationships —
to move in harmony
with the truth you now hold?

Let the answers unfold naturally.
Let them rise from your core.
There's no need to rush or force them.
Simply be open to hear.

Embracing Your True Authentic Self

Until now, your journey
has been one of breaking through —
shattering old habits, fears, narratives, or ignorance.
But here, the work shifts.

It's no longer about pushing with force.
It's about allowing.
Not crafting a new self —
but revealing the one that is already you.

You may notice:
A sharper sense of your boundaries,
your desires taking clearer shape.
A refusal to wear masks
that no longer fit.
A compassion toward the parts of you
that once knew only survival.
And gratitude —
not for an easy path,
but for how the struggle
carved you into someone more authentic.

Apotheosis isn't a destination.
It's a permission.
To live from the inside out.
To stop performing —
and start *living*.

The Gift of Self-Awareness

This is the moment when self-knowledge shifts
from concept to clarity.
You begin to see yourself —
not as a notion,
but as a living reality.

You come to recognize:
Your enduring strengths —
hard-won, deeply rooted.
Your authentic values —
not those you were pressed to pursue,
but the ones that resonate like home.
Your purpose —
perhaps still taking shape,
more outline than blueprint.
Your limits —
not as flaws,
but as the contours
of your humanity.

This clarity lifts the fog.
And once you see your life clearly,
the next steps don't feel like leaps of faith —
they become the natural path forward.
Because they are yours.

The Death of the Old Self

Every transformation demands release —
a kind of death,
not of body,
but of burdens carried too long.

It's the shedding of masks,
worn-out roles,
and guarded layers
that once shielded you,
but now confine your growth.

Allow yourself to grieve them.
Even these false selves had their purpose —
they carried you through,
helped you fit,
helped you endure.

But their time has passed.
You no longer need
their weight to navigate the world.

You've earned the freedom
to stand unarmored,
to greet life
not as the person you were molded to be —
but as the one you've uncovered,
authentic and whole.

Living with Purpose

In this newfound space,
purpose stakes a ground —
not as a fixed structure,
but as a quiet pull toward what feels true.

Your focus sharpens.
Your decisions gain precision.
The full path may remain unseen —
yet what matters now shines crystal clear.
And that clarity is enough
to step forward,
renewed.

Ask yourself:
What feels essential now?
What can I set down — with care, with finality?
How will I honor this new chapter —
not just in thought,
but in the way I meet each day?

Purpose isn't a destination to hunt.
It's a practice to breathe into,
a rhythm to weave
into the fabric of your life.

Key Insight

This is more than a life changed —
it's a re-centering of the soul.
Pain transmutes into meaning.
Doubt yields to deeper understanding.
You're not fleeing your past.
You're weaving it into your unfolding self.
This integration, this steady return to your essence —
is what makes you whole.

Action Step: Ground the Insight

Transformation can fade
unless it's tethered to something solid.
Anchor this moment in a deliberate act.

Choose one way to make it real:

Write a letter to the self you once were.
Honor your endurance,
recognize your burdens,
and release what no longer belongs.

Or draft a vision of who you're becoming —
not a distant ambition,
but a truth already stirring within you.

Or mark this shift with a ritual:
Light a candle to illuminate your path.
Bury a token of what you've outgrown.
Carry a small reminder —
a note, a symbol, a memento —
of what you've reclaimed.

Let this act be your pledge:
To hold fast
to the self you're discovering —
and to remember
why it matters.

The Foundation of Your Truth

This journey doesn't make you perfect.
It shapes you into your truest self.
And once you stand here —
there's no slipping back
to old patterns,
to the person you've outgrown.

You'll move through the world anew —
with greater intention,
with unflinching honesty,
with a presence that is undeniably you.

This is your new foundation.
Let it hold you.
Let it steady your steps.
Let it be the origin
from which the rest of your life begins.

2.7 The Ultimate Boon: Claiming Your Reward

The journey has tested you,
unmade you,
recast you.
And now —
you stand transformed.

Not merely altered,
but reborn in your own truth.
This is the moment of the *Boon*.
Not a final destination,
but a sacred threshold.
The harvest of all you've faced, chosen,
and become.

In myth, the hero claims the treasure,
rescues the captive,
grasps the holy relic.
In life, the reward is subtler —
profound, far more lasting.
It may not match the prize you first imagined.
Yet it's the truth your spirit sought.

It might appear as:
A steady, unshakable confidence.
A purpose that pulses with meaning.
A rediscovered sense of your own worth.

You've earned this —
not simply by reaching the summit,
but by becoming someone
who could.

So what exactly have you earned?
The answer may surprise you,
for it bears little resemblance
to what you initially sought.

Defining the Boon

The boon is the heart's treasure,
born from the journey's trials —
not glittering gold, fleeting fame,
or momentary praise,
but a deeper, lasting reward.

It's the verity you clawed your way to unearth,
the resilience you discovered in your bones,
the calm peace of living true to your essence.

It is both a gift and a responsibility:
not only something to hold,
but a light to carry forward into your days.

The boon might manifest as:
A quiet certainty that steadies your steps.
A vision that burns brighter than doubt.
An inner freedom,
tied not to achievements,
but to the self you've dared to embrace.

It's the moment you realize
the journey didn't just change your path —
it changed how you walk it,
with intention,
with courage,
with a veracity that's now yours to steward.

Recognizing the True Reward

At the outset,
your journey may have chased outward aims —
achievement, approval, connection, escape.
But the real treasure
is what has awakened within you.

It's the insight and wisdom you now hold,
the vision you can't unlearn,
the newfound strength forged
to meet whatever comes next.

It might feel as:
A gentler way of seeing yourself.
A lightness,
freed from burdens long carried in silence.
The boldness to declare your essence,
even when your words waver.
A harmony with what drives you —
your convictions,
your voice,
your vision.

These are not mere fallbacks.
They are the true riches —
not the kind that glitters —
but the kind that *guides*.

Once claimed,
they cannot be stripped away.
They ask only to be lived.

Key Insight

    The true gift of transformation
    lies not in what you sought —
    but in what you awakened within yourself.
    Tenacity. Courage. Faith.
    Not trophies, but inner truths.
    Not bestowed, but earned.
    They belong to you now,
    not as a wish granted,
    but as a strength you've claimed.

Celebrate and Integrate

Pause here — don't hasten past this moment.
It is hallowed.
A quiet bridge
between the self you've left behind
and the one now rising.

Celebration isn't sheer revelry —
it's a tribute to the distance you've traveled.
Integration isn't about flawless execution —
it's about embodying the lessons you've learned.

Let this moment settle.
Let it sharpen your vision.

Reflect:
How have I changed?
What strength did I uncover that once felt out of reach?
What insights now pulse within, impossible to unlearn?

This is not the journey's end.
But it is the point
where your remaking becomes irrevocable,
becoming not just a milestone —
but a way of living.

Reflection Prompt

Pause to look inward —
consider the inner and outer ripples of your journey.
What has shifted in how you see yourself?
In what ways has this shift
redefined what holds the deepest meaning for you?
Who in your circle
might be touched by the insight you now hold?
And how can you begin to live these changes —
through subtle gestures or daring steps?

Let your answers emerge slowly.
They're not forced declarations.
They're your new principles.

Sharing the Boon

The hero's journey doesn't end with personal growth.

Its true depth lies in what you offer to others.
Transformation becomes legacy
when it's shared.

You now carry something powerful:
Insight carved from struggle.
Strength honed through trials.
Truth born of your courage.

These are not just keepsakes.
They are gifts to be shared.

Whether through service,
through creation,
through leadership —
or simply through the steady grace
of how you move through the world —
your story becomes a balm for others.

Ask yourself:
Who might be waiting for the wisdom I now hold?
How could my journey ripple outward —
as healing, as inspiration,
as quiet permission to rise?

The deepest reward
is not only what you've claimed.
It's what you're now prepared
to pay forward.

Closing Reflection

This is the treasure you carry forward —
not just a sharper mind or a bolder spirit,
but a life rooted in authenticity.

You've walked through fire,
not to escape the world,
but to rejoin it with a gift worth sharing.

Let your deeds proclaim
not only the trials you've overcome,
but the insights you've unearthed
on the perilous journey.

Let your presence serve as a gentle summons —
to hope,
to restoration,
to truth.

You've claimed the boon.
Now, let its ripples spread.

But claiming the boon is not the journey's end —
it's the moment when one spiral completes
and another begins to swirl.

The Cycle Continues

The boon is not the journey's end —
it's the threshold to a new beginning.
You don't return to your life as you left it.
You carry something vital now:
insights carved from struggle,
resilience shaped by trials,
a steadier faith in the self you're becoming.

You bring wisdom lifted from the depths.
Here, transformation gets a second wind —
not as an idea,
but as a lived practice.
It colors how you move,
how you lead,
how you love.

The call to adventure brought you here —
and it will call again.
New questions will rise,
new challenges will beckon,
new invitations will summon growth.

But you are no longer the same.
You step into the unknown now
not as a novice, untested or unguarded,
but with strengths earned through the fire:
endurance,

discernment,
boldness,
a purpose that stands firm
against the waves of doubt.

This is no return to where you started.
It's a spiral upward —
a living rhythm of growth,
surrender,
and renewal.

The journey weaves, never straight,
layered with depth,
pulsing with life.
With each turn,
you meet yourself more truly.

No longer just the greenhorn wanderer,
you are becoming your own wise guide.

Living the Boon

You didn't stumble into this moment.
You chose it —
with brave, imperfect, luminous choices —
crossing thresholds
most never dare to approach.

You stayed when retreat felt easier.
You tuned in
when your inner voice pierced through the noise.
You sat with fear.
Gave space to truth.
Showed up for your own unfolding —
even when no one else could witness it.

Now, you hold something rare.
Not a perfect life.
Not every answer.
But a profound sense of who you are.
A voice that rings clearer.
A power that stands firm.

These are the true treasures —
not trophies to display,
but truths to embody.

The boon isn't simply something to have and to hold.
It's part of who you are still becoming.
Let it guide your actions.
Let it shine through your words.
Let it weave itself into the way you live.

The Fire That Transforms

You've journeyed through the wilds of uncertainty,
confronted trials that summoned your courage.

You've been stretched, undone, reborn —
and in that unraveling,
found pieces of yourself you never knew were there.

This is the heart of the journey.
Not just a moment of arrival —
but a crucible of change.

The Initiation phase is where desire
becomes devotion.
Hope ceases to be a fleeting thought,
becoming a truth you live and breathe.
Here —
in the heat of struggle,
in the forging of your spirit —
you touch something transcendent.

You've let go of old certainties.
Challenged inherited beliefs.
Faced your shadows
and embraced the light within.
You've stumbled, no doubt.
But you've grown, undeniably.
And if you're truthful with yourself —
you've become more fully you than ever before.

Through these chapters, you've discovered:
Falling, and then rising again is a wisdom all its own.

Support finds you
when you dare to admit you need it.
Temptation speaks loudest
when you stand on the brink of transformation.
The greatest reward isn't something you grasp —
it's a spark you ignite within yourself
and share with those around you.

This is not the end of your work.
But something irreversible has taken root.
You are not the same person
who stepped into the unknown.
You've earned understanding,
carved out new capabilities,
and caught a glimpse
of your boundless potential.

So pause here.
Honor the effort it took to get to this point.
Let that recognition anchor you —
not in pride,
but in presence.

What follows is not a return to what was.
It's a homecoming —
carrying all you've gained.
Your next step isn't merely forward.

It's toward the life you deserve
and are ready to claim.

Reflection Prompt

What have you uncovered about yourself
on this journey —
a strength, a belief, a trust you didn't know you held?
How will you integrate this discovery into your life —
not only in thought,
but as a guiding force in your actions?
Who or what will anchor you to this new self —
especially when old shadows and doubts
whisper their return?

Let the answers rise gently.
They need not be forced —
only true.

Action Step

Select one insight, strength, or practice
unearthed in this chapter of your journey.
Write it down.
Name it clearly —
as if christening a keepsake
to carry into your future.

Then commit:
Not just to recall it now and then,
but to let it steer your path.
Let it sculpt your next chapter —
not as a distant memory,
but as a living thread
woven into how you move forward.

The Lifepath Forged

You've traveled far —
not only through ideas or concepts,
but across the rugged landscape
of your own becoming.

What began as a distant call
has woven itself into your lifepath.
What once felt fragile and uncertain
has solidified into lived truth.
What you once sought outside yourself —
courage, wisdom, purpose —
now pulses from within,
a flame kindled by your trials.

The next chapter doesn't demand a new beginning.
It calls for a return —
not to the self you left behind,
but as one who's walked through the eye of the storm
and emerged whole,
carrying the weight of hard-earned gifts.

Let these truths shape your steps,
your words,
your vision of the world.
Let them guide how you meet each day —
with presence,
with intention,
with the strength of someone who knows their worth.

The journey stretches onward —
and you, transformed,
move with it,
ready for what it will ask next.

6

COMING HOME

Your hand hesitates on the doorknob —
the same door you've turned a thousand times,
yet now it feels foreign beneath your palm.
Behind this threshold waits the life you left,
Unchanged,
while you carry the weight of new worlds within you.

Every journey circles back to its origin.
Yet the return from the Hero's Journey
is no gentle homecoming.
It carries a certain kind of weight,
a tension —
the gravity of stepping back into a space
that no longer fits the person you've become.

After the trials that tested you,
the reckonings that reshaped you,
the revelations that lit your path —
you pause at the edge of reentry.
As you stand on the *Threshold of Return*.
A quiet resistance stirs.
Hesitation not of fear,
but the gravity of your transformation.

You are not who you were.
The world you left, though,
remains unchanged —
its rhythms, its expectations,
still tethered to the old version of you.

The question rises:
How do you carry this new self
into a place that still calls for the past?

This is where the hardest test unfolds.
Transformation isn't complete
until it breathes in the ordinary.
You may long to linger in the clarity you've found —
the wisdom, the calm, the purpose you've unearthed.
But life doesn't wait for you to settle.
It demands you live it.

The return isn't just stepping back.
It's bringing forward —
the insight you've gained,
the strength you've forged,
the light you found in the shadows.
This phase asks you to embody your truth
amid the familiar,
to walk as the person you've become
in a world that may not yet see you.

The Magic Flight: Holding the Treasure

The return is seldom seamless.
It may stir reluctance,
even a pang of disillusionment.
Those around you may not grasp
the depths you've traversed,
the ways you've transformed.

You might feel adrift —
out of rhythm with the familiar,
misaligned with thresholds you've crossed
that others cannot see.
Tempted, perhaps,
to slip back into roles
you've long since outgrown.

This is the *Magic Flight* —
the test of safeguarding your treasure
amid the pull of old tides.

Changing within is one feat.
Holding that change —
while old dynamics, pressures,
and patterns tug at your past self —
is another.

Yet this moment is vital.
Integration bridges insight to action,
and understanding to character.
Here, transformation sheds its private shell —
becoming the pulse of how you live.

The Freedom to Live: Reinventing Your Path

The return is more than simple reentry.
It's a reinvention.
You move through your world anew —
not detached from it,
but more deeply rooted in its currents.

No longer bound by outdated narratives,
you're guided by stories freshly woven.
You've tasted liberation —
and now, you're poised to embody it.

Joseph Campbell called this *The Freedom to Live* —
a life defined not by perfection,
but by presence.
Growth ceases to be a chase —
it becomes the way you meet each moment.

Here, your next adventure begins.
The hero's journey isn't a single arc.
It spirals — circling back, ever deepening.
Each return brings richer insight,
greater compassion,
and a broader capacity to uplift —
not only yourself,
but those whose paths cross yours

You've fought your demons.
You've survived the threshold.
You've claimed the boon.
Now unfolds the all-important question:
How will you live the wisdom you've gained?

3.1 The Refusal to Return: When Growth Feels Too Big for the Life You Left Behind

After braving the flames and facing your shadows,
after healing and revelation,
there comes a disorienting
moment of contemplation —
the pause before the return.

You've transformed.
Not merely in fleeting ways,
but in the depths of who you are.
Wiser now.
Steadier.

Perhaps softer —
yet profoundly grounded.

Then you look back at the life you left behind —
the old roles, routines, relationships —
and something within you hesitates.

Returning might seem straightforward.
Slip back into the old world.
Pick up the threads where they fell.
Smile, nod, carry on.
But something deeper whispers:
Not yet.
Not as before.

The soul knows what the mind resists —
that true return requires courage
to be misunderstood,
to stand in your truth
even when others call for the familiar.

This hesitation isn't a sign of failure.
It's a sacred pause —
a realization that your growth
has outgrown the frame of your past.

Do you remember the first call —
how it whispered, then demanded,
then finally dragged you from comfort?

You resisted then, too.
You made excuses, delayed, doubted.
But something deeper knew the truth:
you were meant for more.
Now the call sounds again —
not to leave, but to return
carrying everything you've learned.

To illustrate this:
Consider Sarah, returning from a year abroad.
She stands in her childhood bedroom,
surrounded by posters of who she used to be.
Her family expects the same daughter who left —
chatty, eager to please, quick to shrink.
But she's learned to value her own voice,
to speak slowly, to take up space.
The disconnect feels like wearing shoes
two sizes too small.

The Nature of the Refusal

Joseph Campbell named this moment
The Refusal to Return —
a phase where the hero, newly reshaped,
pauses before stepping back into the world
that once defined them.

In your journey,
this reluctance might emerge as:
Hesitation to re-engage with old and familiar spaces.

Fear of being misunderstood or dismissed.
Doubt that your new self will be accepted —
or even recognized.

You've done the inner work.
You've earned this evolution.
Yet now, you're called to return to the same world —
one that once saw you small?
Where your old desk still holds the same scratches,
where familiar voices carry the same expectations,
where the very air seems thick
with memories of who you used to be?

That's no easy ask.
It's a tension between who you've become
and the echoes of who you were expected to be.

Common Narratives in This Phase

I've come so far... what if going back unravels it all?
They won't understand the person I've become.
Perhaps I should press forward —
and leave the past behind.
What if I've outgrown this life entirely?
Perhaps the return isn't to where I left,
but to where I'm meant to be.

These thoughts ripple through your mind,
planting doubts into the heart of the journey.

This inner resistance is profoundly human.
It's the voice of a self guarding
what's newly formed —
wary that reentering old spaces
might unravel the growth you've fought to claim.
It's the fear that the world won't embrace
your new self,
that stepping back risks losing what you've gained.

But this isn't weakness.
It's the tender instinct to protect what's precious,
a testament to how far you've traveled,
and how deeply your transformation matters.

Why We Resist the Return

The refusal stems not only from fear —
it's a matter of identity and who you've become.
You've shed the self that once fit neatly
into the contours of your old world.

Returning means confronting the familiar —
people, places, patterns,
still locked in their old shapes,
unchanged while you've already transformed.

There's a quiet dread:
Will this new self be seen?
Or will it be rejected?

The mind whispers:
I've outgrown that life.
What if old habits reclaim me?
Why return if nothing else's changed?

But here's the deeper truth:
The return isn't about going backward.
It's carrying your growth into the light,
bringing the fire of your transformation
to spaces that once felt confining.

It's stepping back into your world —
not as the person you were,
but as the one you're becoming,
bold,
unapologetic,
and unwavering in your truth.

Key Insight

> You didn't change just to endure and survive.
> You changed to live more truthfully —
> with greater authenticity.
> And that truth is meant to ripple outward,
> touching the world around you,
> transforming not just your life,
> but the lives of those you encounter.
> Your becoming is not a private ceremony.
> It's an invitation others will feel,
> even if they cannot name it.

Integration Over Isolation

The pull to retreat
into your transformed self is strong.
To withdraw,
to guard your newfound truth in solitude.
Yet change held secret remains incomplete.
It must be lived,
brought boldly into the world.

This transition calls for reflection.
What corners of your former life
no longer fit the person you've become?
What still carries meaning —
and how can you meet it with fresh eyes?
Where must you draw lines
to safeguard the growth you've earned?

You're not meant to conceal who you are now.
You're called to embody it —
to let your transformation breathe,
to let it shape how you move,
connect,
and stand in the world.

Action Step: Your Return Plan

Growth unshared leads only to isolation.
Don't retreat into your evolution.
Step back into the world with intention.

Start by charting the terrain.
Which places, people, or moments
might test your new self?
Name what you'll hold firm.
What practices or limits will anchor your growth?

Create a return mantra —
a single phrase to steady you when old doubts tug.
For example:
I step forward as the person I've become —
and that is my strength.

Let this plan guide you,
not as a shield,
but as a compass for living your truth.

After completing this practice,
notice what shifts within you.
How does your body feel?
What thoughts arise?
What does this tell you
about\ the changes taking root?

You Are Not Who You Were: Embrace the Change

This phase isn't about masking your transformation.
It's about letting it shine through —
in the cadence of your words,
in the weight of your choices,
in the presence you bring to each moment.

And if the old world no longer fits?
That's as it should be.
The return doesn't always lead back
to where you began.
Sometimes, it propels you toward a new horizon.

You've earned the freedom to live on your own terms.
Don't hold back from claiming it.
And don't withhold from the world
the self it's been waiting to meet.

3.2 The Magic Flight: Overcoming Final Resistance

The journey doesn't end with revelation.
The hardest part is still bringing it home.

You've wandered the depths of your shadows,
endured the weight of trials,
dismantled the chains of old habits.
You've emerged carrying something more real —
a sharper, more grounded sense of who you are.

But now comes a challenge few foresee,
and fewer still prepare for:
the return to your former *ordinary world*.

This is *The Magic Flight* —
yet it often feels far from enchanted.
It's a stage too easily ignored —
the subtle struggle of weaving your growth
into the fabric of a familiar life.

You've changed.
The world you left, though, remains untouched,
still shaped by the shadow of your former self.

Now, you face the task of reconciling
your new truth
with a reality that is still defined by the old you.

When the Old World Meets the New You

You reenter familiar spaces —
the fluorescent hum of your office,
the particular creak of your front door,
the scent of coffee brewing in the morning ritual.
The same routines,
the same faces with their practiced smiles.
Yet you are no longer the person who left them —
your shoulders carry themselves differently now,
your breath moves deeper,
your eyes see what they once missed.

Here lies the quiet tension.
The world may hold you to old expectations,
but your spirit now answers to a higher call —
a fierce commitment to the self you've forged.

This isn't about escaping the past.
It's about redefining how you engage with it.
Not fleeing your surroundings,
but honoring the growth you've claimed within them.

You are no longer bound by what once confined you.
You stand as living proof
that transformation is real —
that change, once thought impossible,
breathes through you now.

Why This Phase Feels Harder Than Expected

Serenity feels unfamiliar
after years tangled in turmoil.
Insight stirs unease
in those still lost in haze and confusion.
Your growth redraws your edges —
and not all will respect the new lines
you've established.

Resistance doesn't vanish with your transformation.
It shifts, taking new forms and evolves.

Doubt cloaks itself as reason.
Shame murmurs you've dared too far,
changed too much.
The pull of the familiar beckons —
even when it no longer fits you.

You may ponder the nagging question:
How do I live this new self in a world
still expecting the old me?

Key Insight

This phase isn't a relapse —
it's a crucible for weaving your growth into life.
It's not enough to understand the lessons.
You must live them —
especially when it feels daunting,
when the world pulls you toward old paths,
and change feels heavier than you imagined.
True transformation roots itself here —
not in insight alone,
but in the act of becoming.

The Tests of Transformation

You've set your limits firm —
yet loved ones press against them.
You've made peace with old wounds —
until a chance encounter tears them open.

You've chosen to grow —
and still, temptation slips in,
cloaked in fresh allure,
subtler, more seductive than before.

These aren't signs of failure.
They're evidence of your evolution.
Proof you've stepped into a self
that no longer bends to old molds,
even when they beg for your return.

Each challenge affirms it —
you've transcended what once confined you.
Now, the world must meet the person
you've dared to become.

Action Step: Make Your Transformation Tangible

Choose one sphere of your life —
personal, relational, or professional.
This week, let your growth shine through action.

Reflect:
What does it look like to act from my new truth?
What situations are likely to test me —
and how can I prepare?
How can I express my evolution
in my words, my presence, my choices?

Be specific.
Root your change in deliberate steps.
Growth becomes sustainable
when it moves beyond thought,
becoming a visible, living practice
woven into the fabric of your days.

Three times daily, pause and ask:
Am I acting from my new truth
or out of old habits?
What would my transformed self choose here?

Let these moments guide you back to alignment.

Rituals for Reinforcement

You don't need to be perfect —
but you do need to be consistent.
Try these practices to root your transformation:

Morning Anchor

Begin each day by reconnecting with your purpose.
Write it clearly. Speak it boldly.
Feel its weight settle within you,
guiding your steps as you move into the world,
a reminder of the self you're shaping.

Evening Pause
As night falls, reflect:
What choice today honored my integrity?
Celebrate even the smallest victories,
and consider where tomorrow can shine brighter.
This habit builds strength,
weaving your growth into daily life.

Tangible Cues
Place a symbol — a note, a token, an image —
where your eyes will easily find it.
Let it call you back when doubts stir,
grounding you in the essence
of who you've become.
Keep these touchstones near,
visible reminders of your journey.

The Real Danger: Drifting from Focus

The threat you will face isn't surrender —
it's distraction.
You stay busy, productive, helpful.
Yet, subtly, silently, you begin to drift.

What looks like progress
becomes a slow erosion —
movement without direction,
motion that carries you further
from the truth you fought to claim.

Distractions might look like:
Slipping back into familiar roles or ties,
comfortable but misaligned with who you've become.
Filling your days with tasks,
using activity to dodge deeper inner work.
Chasing new goals or projects,
as a way to avoid finishing the one that truly matters,
the one that will bring you closer to your true self.

These don't always feel like sabotage or betrayal.
But they are.
They scatter your focus —
and sap your strength.

Take Marcus, who spent years saying *yes*
to every request, every invitation.
Through therapy, he learned to honor his own needs.
Now, at his first family gathering post-recovery,
his aunt asks him to organize the reunion.
The old Marcus would have smiled and agreed.
The new Marcus feels his chest tighten,
hears the familiar voice: *"Just say yes, it's easier."*

This is his magic flight moment —
will he guard his hard-won boundaries
or slip back into the comfortable prison of approval?

Movement is not progress.
True alignment demands focus,
and the resolve to stay devoted
to what stirs your deepest purpose.

Reconnect with Your Purpose

When resistance surges —
as it surely will —
return to your foundation.

Ask:
What ignited this journey in the first place?
What fierce longing, what quiet spark or deep desire,
first called me to this path?
What truth would I forsake if I turned away now?
What would I leave behind —
not just today,
but for the life I'm building?
What part of myself am I guarding by pressing on?
Who am I shaping to be by choosing to move forward,
even when the path grows steep?

Capture these answers on paper.
Let them take root in ink,
anchoring you to your deepest intent.
Speak them aloud.
Let your voice carry the weight of your commitment,
echoing the reasons you began
and the purpose that drives you still.

These truths are your armor.
They will fortify you against doubt,
against fear,
against the temptation to retreat.

You Are Not Backsliding: You're Being Forged

If weariness weighs heavy,
if doubt clouds your path,
or the urge to retreat pulls strong —
this is not defeat.
This is the fire of becoming.

You aren't unraveling.
You're being refined,
molded by the very trials you meet.

This is the rite of passage:
not merely grasping transformation —
but breathing it into your life.

Pause, if you need.
Breathe deep, let the moment steady your heart.
But don't turn back.
Don't slip into the ease of old ways,
no matter how they beckon.

You are not the person you left behind.
You are not adrift.
You are on the cusp of home.

The journey nears its close,
and with every step,
you draw closer to the self
you were always destined to be.

But even the strongest among us
need not walk alone —
wisdom knows when to lean into support.

3.3 The Rescue from Without: Embracing Support for Reintegration

Even the mightiest of heroes don't return unassisted.
In myth, this is the moment when a guiding force —
a divine spark, a steadfast friend,
or an unforeseen ally —
steps in, not to bear the hero's load,
but to light the way toward the journey's end.

It's a profound reminder:
transformation doesn't forge you into stone —
it deepens your humanity,
tying you closer to the truth of your path.

You've braved the depths,
confronted your fears,
claimed your inner fire.

Yet, as you turn toward home,
you may feel adrift —
suspended between a life you've outgrown
and a self you're still learning to inhabit.

The clarity you fought for may waver,
and lacing your growth into life may feel exhausting.

This is where connection and support
become vital —
not as a crutch, but as a steady hand,
a voice to remind you that your strength, though vast,
doesn't mean you have to walk alone.

The Power of Accepting Help

This journey was never meant to be solitary.
Just as guides, mentors, or allies emerged
when the path grew daunting,
others now arrive to share the task
of fusing your transformation into life.

Remember your first mentors —
how they appeared
exactly when you needed them most,
offering not answers, but better questions?

They taught you to trust the process,
to lean into uncertainty.
Their gift wasn't dependence, but discernment —
knowing when to stand alone
and when to reach for a steady hand.
That wisdom guides you now.

Embracing their support isn't weakness.
It's a thoughtful choice —
the understanding that growth thrives
not only in isolation,
but through bonds, shared journeys,
and collective strength.

Support rarely arrives with grand gestures.
More often, it slips in quietly,
in tender, unassuming moments:
A friend who holds space,
listening without judgment.
A stranger whose smile arrives
exactly when doubt clouds your vision.
A book that falls open to the page
your soul needed to read.
A fleeting act of kindness,
whispering: *you're not alone.*

Sometimes, the rescue is simply
someone's faith in you,
steadying you when your own belief falters.

A colleague who notices your growth
and reflects it back with genuine admiration.
A mentor who lights the way to your next step.
A community that reflects your evolution,
showing you the courage
you might overlook in yourself.

Why We Resist Support

Modern culture worships self-sufficiency,
teaching us that standing alone is power,
and leaning on others signals frailty.

Yet true strength blooms in connection —
in knowing when to reach out,
in daring to be seen, raw and real.
Not to be embarrassed by vulnerability,
and trusting others to reflect the strength
you might miss in yourself.

You may hesitate to seek support because:
You fear your new self won't be understood.
You dread appearing weak or dependent.
You question whether anyone can grasp your path.

But here's the deeper reality:
We all crave empathy
that reinforces our self-confidence.

We all need moments
when someone holds up a light,
reminding us who we've become
when our own vision falters.

Consider Maya, who learned in couples therapy
to voice her needs without blame,
to listen without defending.

She returns home excited to practice
these new ways of connecting.
But when her partner Jake snaps about dinner plans,
her old self would have snapped back
or swallowed her hurt in silence.
Instead, she breathes and says,
"I hear that you're stressed. What do you need right now?"
Jake pauses, confused by her calm response.
"You're being weird," he says. "Just... normal weird."

Maya realizes her growth means nothing
if she can't help Jake feel safe enough
to meet her in this new space.
She needs his partnership in building
the relationship they both deserve —
not perfect understanding,
but willingness to try something different.

Key Insight
Even the boldest heroes need a hand —
not as a sign of defeat,

but because weaving change into life is a collective act.
Transformation triggers within,
yet it blooms fully through connection.
It is in community, in support, in being truly seen,
your inner shift lands,
and your journey finds its deepest impact.

Action Step: Build Your Circle of Support

Pause to assess your network with care.
And ask:
Who celebrates my growth without diminishing it?
Who truly listens —
holding space rather than rushing to solve?
Who challenges me with love, not judgment?

Then consider:
Have you welcomed these allies into your journey?
Have you allowed their support
to lighten your load —
or are you still bearing it alone?

Reaching out is not a sign of weakness.
It's a mark of strength.
It's the understanding that transformation
thrives in connection,
growing richer through shared bonds.
The hand you extend toward others
is the same one that pulls you forward.

Embracing Shared Strength

The "rescue" isn't yielding.
It's inviting others to walk with you.
It's letting go of the need to always stand tall,
always certain, always composed and unshaken.

Allowing support is a bold act of courage.
It affirms a profound truth:
Healing happens not in solitude,
but in the warmth of relations.

The companions who walked beside you
through the valley of transformation
remain with you now —
some in memory, some in presence,
all woven into who you've become.

This is how your transformation takes hold —
not only through the lessons you've learned,
but through the hands that steady you,
the hearts that see and nurture your growth.

So, when the path grows heavy,
when integrating change feels daunting,
don't tighten your grip.
Reach out.
Let someone remind you:
You've come far —
and you were never meant to carry this alone.

3.4 The Crossing of the Return Threshold: Embodying Your Wisdom

Stepping back into your world can unsettle
more than the journey itself.
You've traversed vast inner terrains,
faced the shadows you once hid,
and claimed the strength of your truth.

Now, the new challenge looms:
Can you live that truth
in a world that once muted your voice?

This is the *Crossing of the Return Threshold* —
where wisdom turns into action.
Transformation in solitude, ritual,
or reflection is one thing.
Carrying it into the spaces, relationships,
and rhythms that shaped your past is another.

Here, change solidifies.
Here, your lessons begin to breathe through you.
Here, growth shifts from thought to instinct,
then to action,
becoming the pulse of how you live.

Consider this:
Elena returns to her corporate role
after a leadership retreat that cracked her open.

She's learned that vulnerability is strength,
that listening matters more than having answers.
But her team expects the old Elena —
decisive, commanding, always in control.
Her first meeting becomes a crucible:
Does she lead from her new understanding
or retreat to the armor of old authority?

When she admits she doesn't have all the answers
and asks for input,
the room shifts.
Some colleagues seem confused,
others breathe a sigh of relief.
And most welcome the change.
This is transformation living in the ordinary.

The Tension Between Old and New

You stand poised between two realms:
the familiar world you left behind —
and the vibrant self you've begun to uncover.

This friction is raw — and essential.
It's where past and present collide,
revealing what no longer fits.

You've stared into the abyss before —
faced the parts of yourself
you swore you'd never acknowledge.

That courage serves you now
as you confront a different darkness:
the fear that your light
might be too bright for this world.
But you've learned shadows aren't enemies —
they're simply places
that haven't met your truth yet.

You might find yourself hesitating
before entering rooms that once felt like home,
or choosing silence in conversations
that used to fill your hours.
This isn't retreat —
it's discernment.

Old roles pinch like outgrown garments —
tight across the chest where your heart has expanded,
binding at the wrists where your hands
have learned to reach for different things,
the fabric rough against skin
that's grown tender with self-compassion.

Familiar exchanges skim the surface,
missing the depths you now carry.
Your surroundings may no longer mirror
the inner landscape you've cultivated,
and that dissonance can unsettle,
stirring isolation, frustration, even doubt
in your new self.

Yet this isn't about slipping back
into the past as you were.
It's about stepping forward —
seeing with new eyes,
acting with purpose,
living in harmony with the truth you've claimed.

Key Insight
    The return isn't a retreat to your former self —
    it's reclaiming your place in the world
    with a sharper, deeper awareness.
    You carry your wisdom forward —
    not as a badge of honor,
    but as a living truth,
    forged in experience,
    woven into every choice you make.

Practical Integration: Living Your Change

To cross the return threshold with purpose,
your inner transformation must ripple
into your outer world.

Begin here:

Redefine What Matters
Craft aspirations that echo your deepest values,
not the faded dogmas you once followed.

Speak Your Truth
Express your evolution with honesty,
even if others struggle to see the self you've claimed.

Guard Your Spirit
Not every person, not every demand,
earns a place in this new chapter of you.
Set boundaries that honor the person
you're becoming.

Anchor Through Rituals
Build small, daily practices to ground your growth —
moments that tether you to the lessons you've earned.

Integration doesn't happen overnight.
It's an ongoing process —
to live your truth,
to weave your wisdom into each choice,
step by deliberate step.

Action Step: Crafting Your Re-Entry Plan

Select one sphere of your life
to step back into with purpose:
relationships, work, health, creativity, or spirituality.

Reflect:
What wisdom have I gained that belongs in this space?
What must change to honor the person I am now?
How can I move forward with poise, courage, and clarity?

Write these thoughts clearly.
Then, within the next day, take one tangible step
to bring your transformation to life.
It might be a heartfelt conversation,
a boundary firmly set,
a new ritual started,
or a decision that reflects your growth.

Create a *Threshold Ritual* —
a small ceremony marking your reentry.
Light a candle, speak your intention aloud,
or plant something that will grow
as your new life takes root.
Let this moment cement your commitment
to living your transformation.

Be prepared to face challenges and setbacks,
and learn from them to strengthen your resolve.
Maintain a positive attitude and focus on the benefits
of achieving your goals.

Let your life become a canvas for your change.
Make it seen.
Make it real.
Make it congruent.

Embracing the Ordinary with New Eyes

The world may appear unchanged —
yet you step through it differently.

You've become someone who:
Chooses a thoughtful response over snappy reflex.
Prioritizes honesty over approval.
Upholds your essence, even when it's inconvenient.

The hero doesn't return untouched.
You return awake —
and that awakening sparks a quiet revolution
in every life you touch.

You don't need to announce your change.
You need only to live it.
Let your presence carry what words cannot,
for it's in your choices, your tenacity,
your way of being
that the depth of your transcendence shines.

This is the gift of your journey:
To return to your life —
and feel, at last, that you belong.
Not as one straining to fit in,
but as one who has claimed their place,
living the life they were always destined to embrace.

3.5 Master of Two Worlds: Balancing Growth and Presence

After the descent, the revelation, and the return —
a moment arrives
when you no longer straddle divided worlds.
The inner labor is complete.
You've confronted your shadows,
released what no longer fits,
and embraced a truer self.

But transformation doesn't mean escaping the world.
It means engaging it fully —
holding fast to the essence you've uncovered.

This is the art of *Integration*:
Not chasing an unattainable ideal —
but living with authenticity and purpose
in your relationships, responsibilities,
and everyday moments,
without forsaking who you've become.

It's standing at the heart of your life,
feeling at home within it,
even as it shifts and unfolds in unexpected ways.

Integration isn't about abandoning
the world you knew.

It's about reentering it with a fuller presence —
not to conform, but to expand within it,
bringing your truth to every corner you touch.

Weaving Both Worlds

You no longer stand divided
between the self you were and the self you've become.
The journey isn't about choosing one over the other,
but blending them into a vibrant whole —
a tapestry that honors every thread of your being.

You've died before —
not physically, but utterly.
The old self had to shatter
for this one to emerge.

You remember the terror of that dissolution,
the grief of releasing who you thought you were.
Now you understand:
that death was not an ending
but a graduation
into this fuller way of being.

You don't reject the world you knew —
you engage it with fresh eyes,
meeting it from a place
of deeper insight and awareness.

You can step into life's currents
without being swept away.
You can dance with chaos
while holding your center,
bend with the wind
yet remain rooted in your truth.
You can care deeply,
yet hold fast to your own heart.
You can give generously,
without draining your spirit.
You can join the pulse of the everyday,
yet stay true to your deepest values,
unswayed by what no longer serves you.

This is the art of balance —
standing grounded in the reality of your life,
while carrying the light of your growth.
Not as a passive observer,
but a deliberate force —
rooted in your hard-earned wisdom,
steadied by your lived truth,
and unmoved by distractions that sway others.

Consider this example:
David discovers meditation after years of anxiety.
He learns to sit with discomfort,
to breathe through overwhelm.
When his teenager slams doors and shouts,
the old David would have matched that energy —
yelling back, asserting control.

But now he stands steady,
feeling his feet on the ground,
his breath moving slowly.
He responds instead of reacting.
"I can see you're upset.
I'm here when you're ready to talk."
His daughter's anger hits his calm
and transforms into tears, then conversation.
This is mastery — not perfection,
but grounded presence in the storm.

You're not here to be carried by the current.
You're here to move with intention —
to shape the waters you walk through,
and let the real you
be seen in every ripple.

Key Insight

True mastery lies in blending your worlds.
It's not about erasing your past
or guarding your growth in secret.
It's about weaving them together —
the lessons carved from yesterday
and the wisdom born of your journey —
into a life lived with authenticity.
It's moving through each day
with a heart wide open,
where every choice, every moment,
reflects the depth of who you are
and the self you're still becoming.

Signs You're Entering This Phase

You may be crossing into this stage when:
You find calm amid turmoil —
not by avoiding the tempest,
but by keeping faith to your own truth.

You move through familiar places
with fresh insight and confidence,
carrying a quiet strength that shapes your path.

You lean on your inner guide,
trusting it over the voices of doubt or distraction,
heeding the wisdom that rises within.

You act with purpose —
no longer swayed by old impulses,
but choosing each step with intention and care.

You no longer seek the world
to validate your growth —
because you live it,
your presence and purpose resounding
louder than any external approval ever could.

Living Authentically in Everyday Life

Mastery isn't the end of growth.

It's learning to evolve
while holding fast to your essence.
To expand
while staying grounded in who you are.

It looks like:
Acting true to yourself,
even in quiet moments
when no eyes are upon you.
Saying *No* with kindness —
free of guilt,
drawing lines that protect your journey,
even when it stings.
Speaking your truth without needing to defend it —
feeling the words rise from your belly,
steady and warm,
your voice carrying new weight,
letting it stand in the silence that follows,
rooted in sincerity,
not a hunger for approval.
Embracing your values and worth,
not as a performance,
but as a quiet strength
that speaks through your presence.

This isn't about outshining others.
It's about being wholly you —
neither shrinking to fit old molds
nor raising your voice to be noticed.

Action Step: Live Your Life with Intention

Having returned from the fault lines
of your former self —
what has emerged, and how will you honor it?
The treasure you carry is not meant for display —
it's meant to be lived, daily, in choices
only you can make.

Reflect:
What daily habits will keep me tethered
to what now feels authentic and true?
What rituals will ground me in my essence,
even when the world tugs me elsewhere?
Where can I carve out room
for both evolving and simply being,
balancing quiet presence with my growth?
How will I infuse intention —
not just effort — into my days,
choosing focus over frenzy, purpose over noise?
In what small ways can I honor this new self
in how I love, lead, and live?
How can my choices reflect who I've become,
without the need to prove it to others?

Write your answers clearly.
Let them sink deep into your soul.
Then, this week, take one deliberate step —
to shape your life around the person you are now,
not the shadow of your former self.

Sharing Your Light

The final phase of the Return isn't about rest —
it's weaving your growth into the fabric of your life.
It's learning to inhabit your transformed self
with grace and purpose.

You carry insights now,
not only to preach, but to practice.
Your wisdom isn't for show —
but for living.

The treasure you sought in distant lands
was never gold or glory.
It was this: the ability to stand
in the center of your own life
and feel at home.
The elixir you claimed in darkness
now flows through ordinary moments —
transforming not just you,
but everyone your presence touches.

You don't need a platform.
Your life is your message.

Be a gentle beacon for those still lost in darkness,
a steady presence for those
who haven't yet found their way.

Extend compassion to those
at their journey's beginning,
with understanding, never judgment.

Let your actions become the subtle invitation,
not the argument.
Live so your presence inspires others to step forward,
without forcing them to follow.

You are the bridge now —
between inner growth and outer impact,
between the healed self within
and a world still finding its way to wholeness.

This is true mastery —
not in grand gestures or bold statements,
but in the daily embodiment
of the person you've grown to be.

3.6 Freedom to Live: Purpose and Presence

You've braved storms that reshaped your core,
faced demons you once ignored,
released what no longer held meaning,
and grappled with revelations,
emerging with hard-won insight.

The true gift of this journey lies not only
in what you've gained —
but in how you choose to carry it forward.

This final stage is not a conclusion —
it's a homecoming.
Not to the self you left behind,
but to the one you were destined to embody.

No longer bound by fear,
no longer tied to outdated roles
or inherited expectations,
you stand unburdened,
free to step fully into your new life.

You've earned both the right and the call —
to live with focus, courage, and presence,
to choose from a place of deep intent,
not fleeting impulse.

Here, you're not merely passing through life —
you're giving it purpose,
living the change you sought,
letting it guide your every step.

This is the freedom few ever taste —
not the absence of struggle,
but the presence of choice made conscious.
You move through the world awake now,
sovereign over the story you tell with your days.

The Essence of Freedom

Joseph Campbell named this phase
The Freedom to Live —
a way of being where your life no longer bends
to impulse, avoidance, or doubt.

You move through the world
not to prove your worth,
but to express what's true —
your footsteps finding their own rhythm,
your hands gesturing with quiet confidence,
your presence filling space
without apology or explanation,
a deep, authentic reverence of who you are.

Your actions spring from harmony,
not from duty, demands or expectations,
but from choices that mirror your truest self.

You meet others with kindness —
born from the grace
you've learned to offer yourself,
rooted in acceptance, compassion,
and understanding.

You are free —
not because the world holds no limits,
but because you know your own heart,
and that knowing steadies you,
letting you walk with calm assurance,
unswayed by outside pressures,
grounded in the quintessence you've claimed.

Living Beyond the Journey

The world may remain the same —
yet you are evolved.
You now wield the strength to face uncertainty
without faltering,
to meet conflict without losing your footing,
to hold joy without bracing for its loss.

You've learned to stand steady,
even in the midst of life's storms,
untouched by the chaos that once overwhelmed you.

Your presence becomes your power —
a quiet strength that needs no proof,
radiating in how you carry yourself
through the world.

You no longer chase external validation
in others' approval,
your sense of self rooted so deeply within
that no force can shake it.

Now, you live beyond the journey —
not as one endlessly searching,
but as one anchored in their own essence,
moving through life with poise, grace, and purpose.

Key Shifts That Define This Phase

Presence Over Performance
You no longer seek praise or external validation —
your worth shines through
by simply being who you are.
Your worth isn't tied to achievements or approval,
but to the depth of your presence,
the truth woven into every moment you inhabit.

Purpose Over Perfection
You've let go of chasing an unattainable ideal.
Instead, you stride forward in your truth,
embracing the grace in your flaws.
You move forward not because the future is perfect,
but because it's real —
and it's yours.

Service Over Self-Importance
Your growth isn't yours alone.
It's a beacon, illuminating not only your path,
but offering guidance to others still finding their way.
Your journey ripples outward,
carrying hope, insight, and compassion
to those who share your world.

Key Insight

Freedom isn't the absence of struggle —
it's the strength to stand tall in the storm,
eyes clear, heart steady.
It's choosing serenity over turmoil,
finding quiet amid the noise,
trusting your inner compass
to navigate the terrains of life.
It's choosing focus over chaos,
not by dodging life's messy moments,
but by rooting yourself in what's true,
even when the world feels uncertain.
It's choosing love over fear,
acting from a place of compassion,
rather than retreating into cynicism.
Freedom is not fleeing from challenge —
it's the courage to meet it head-on,
and to thrive within it.

Action Step: Shaping Your Ongoing Journey

You've crossed the threshold.
You've integrated the lessons.
Now begins the deeper work —
living your truth in every moment, every choice.

Reflect:
What practices will keep me anchored in my truth,
especially when the world tries
to pull me in different directions?

How can I turn insight into action —
not just once, but consistently,
so that my evolution becomes a natural part of my life?
Who might benefit from the wisdom I've gained?
How can my journey inspire those still searching?
What does it mean to live with
integrity, presence, and purpose —
even in the ordinary, everyday moments that go unseen?

Craft a **Declaration of Self** —
a brief statement, two to three sentences,
capturing how you will show up
from this moment forward.
Beginning with "I am someone who..."
and completing it with three qualities
that define your transformed essence.
For example: "I am someone who speaks truth
with kindness, chooses growth over comfort,
and trusts my inner wisdom above all else."

Let it be your guide,
a steady light steering your path,
keeping you aligned with the self you're becoming.

Embracing the Next Adventure

The Hero's Journey doesn't conclude here.
It flows onward —
a living current,
evolving with every step you take.

Growth is not linear — it spirals, deepens,
pushing you forward, again and again.
New thresholds will rise,
new shadows will call for your courage,
new revelations will await your discovery.

But now, you carry an unshakable strength:
The map is no longer external.
It's etched within you,
woven into the fabric of your being.
You are no longer searching for a guide —
you carry the light
that guides your own steps.

So breathe. Stand tall.
Feel the ground beneath you,
steadying your pace, reminding you
that you belong here.

This is your life now —
free, awake, yours to shape.
You hold all you need to meet what lies ahead.

When the next call sounds, and it will,
you'll be ready —
not because you have all the answers,
but because you've learned to step forward boldly,
to trust the path as it unfolds with each step,
and to experience the journey fully,
not just chase its end.

Coming Home to Yourself

Returning holds a quiet sanctity.
Not to the past, nor to the place where you first began,
but to the essence of who you've always been —
the self that shines
beneath the noise and distractions,
uncovered beyond the veils
that once dimmed your sight.

You — who walked through darkness and held fast,
swaying like reeds in a wind,
emerging not broken, but fortified,
standing taller than you ever imagined.

The Hero's Journey doesn't close with fanfare,
no cheers, no cascade of light.
What awaits is subtler —
more intimate, more profound.
It's the calm of a spirit no longer at odds with itself —
the settling exhale that reaches your toes,
the softening of shoulders
that once braced against the world,
a peace born from embracing your fullness,
from laying down the fight
and feeling your spine lengthen
with the relief of simply being.

It's the ease of a breath
unburdened by regret,
the freedom to walk the world
without the weight of performance.

To speak with candor.
To live with grace.
To be seen — and let that be enough.

You've crossed many thresholds,
braved the uncharted,
and returned not with trophies,
but with a quieter treasure: truth.

The real gift was never in what you gathered,
but in what you let go.
Not in who you became —
but in stopping to hide who you are.

And now, you step forward anew.
Not as a wanderer seeking answers,
but as one who has found home
in your own skin — awake, present, whole.

The Wisdom of the Knower

You understand that growth and struggle are kin —
not foes, but dance partners,
each leading the other
toward a deeper, richer wisdom.

Fear no longer rules you —
it's a guide, whispering lessons,
urging you onward, not chaining you back.

Love — for yourself, for others, for life itself —
is the golden thread weaving your journey,
guiding you through darkness
into the radiance of truth.

Questions may linger.
Stumbles may come.
But you no longer flee your own heart.
You no longer wait for the perfect moment to begin.
You know that the only moment is now.

This is the strength of living in the present.
Freedom means you're no longer bound
by yesterday —
no longer a prisoner of your past,
lifted by who you've become.
Nor are you enslaved to an uncertain future,
released from fears of what might be,
grounded in the reality of what is.

It means showing up —
boldly, fully,
even when your voice wavers,
even when doubt tries to creep in.

You stand firm,
knowing you are enough just as you are.
You honor your boundaries —
not with walls,
but with space carved for your growth,
unapologetic for the self you've claimed.

You speak with clarity,
walk with presence,
and live each day as if it truly matters —
because it does.
Because you do.

No map is needed now.
You are the guide,
your own North Star,
the steady flame lighting the way,
the voice cheering you on:
Keep going. The journey continues.

Final Reflection: The Endless Spiral

This journey has no finish line.
Only chapters,
only seasons,
only spirals of remembering, losing —
and rediscovering who you are.

This isn't your first return —
you've made this journey before
in smaller ways, quieter moments.
Each time, you bring back
a deeper layer of understanding.

You will hear the call again —
new thresholds to cross,
new challenges to meet.
There will be uncharted caves to enter,
fierce dragons to confront,
hidden wisdom waiting in the shadows,
ready for you to claim.

But now —
you no longer shrink from the dark.
You've faced its depths,
made peace with what dwells there,
and found harmony within yourself.

The fears that once held sway
have lost their grip.
You step forward,
not chasing meaning,
but embodying it with every breath.

You are no longer merely the wanderer.
You are the path itself —
the trail, the journey,
etched into each choice you make.

And wherever the next step leads,
may you walk with purpose.
May you move with presence.
And above all —
may you walk as your most authentic self.

7

AN ODE TO THE HERO WITHIN

Fate whispers to the warrior, 'You can not withstand the storm.'
The warrior whispers back, 'I am the storm'.

Every great journey begins in stillness —
with a quiet question.
A subtle ache.
A restless sense,
woven through the rhythms of ordinary life,
whispering:
Is this all there is?

It doesn't always roar.
Sometimes it quivers,
hiding behind fear,
nestling in longing,
or fading into the weight of unclaimed dreams.

Yet it persists —
beckoning you toward something unseen,
deeper, truer, fiercely alive.

And so, you step forth.
Not with answers, perhaps —
but with courage,
daring to embrace the unknown,
even when the path lies uncertain.

You shed the familiar:
roles, habits, routines, and inherited opinions.
The smaller version of yourself
that once seemed to fit,
but now feels impossibly confining.
You cross a threshold not marked by signs,
defined only by an inner shift —
a vow to no longer live half-awake.

This is the **Departure** —
the Hero's Journey's first breath.
Not flight, but awakening.
You may feel unprepared.
You may stumble.
Yet each step forward is an act of rebellion
against a life lived by default.
Each step is proof:
You are being remade.

Yet the path ahead deepens,
calls you further inward.
What began as brave steps
now asks for transformation —
not just of circumstance, but of soul.

But rebirth requires more
than crossing thresholds.
It demands you meet yourself
in the depths,
where real change begins.

Then comes the **Initiation** —
where you are not merely tested,
but forged anew.
The road offers no easy shortcuts.
Trials will greet you.
Distractions will tempt you.
Your own shadows will rise, unflinching.

But with every hurdle, illusions crumble.
With every wound acknowledged,
a deeper truth emerges.
You're not here to prove your worth —
you're here to reclaim it.
Not breaking,
but being shaped,
like steel in fire,
tempered by the heat of your resolve.

In this crucible of transformation,
allies appear unbidden.
You uncover strengths you never knew you had.
Meet the part of you that refuses to give up —
not now,
or ever again.

You confront old narratives,
ingrained fears,
the silence once carved by shame.
And gradually —
through grit and effort,
through grace and through sheer endurance —
you arrive at something more authentic.
Not perfect,
but whole.
Not yet complete,
but true.

And then — the **Return.**
Perhaps the steepest climb of all.
Not the leaving, nor the enduring,
but the reentry into a world that is unchanged —
while you are already transformed.

Carrying wisdom in open hands,
you wonder where to lay it down,
how to share it.

This is where the journey asks for integration —
not just to hold change,
but to live it,
to breathe it into every moment.

Now you see: the journey was never about escape.
It was about coming home —
with clearer eyes, a braver heart,
the strength to live anew.

You become a bridge —
spanning the self you were
and the self still unfolding.
You walk in both worlds:
honoring your past,
embodying your growth,
quietly uplifting others toward their own light.

This is the Hero's Journey.
Your journey.
It doesn't end here.
It renews —
in the small acts of courage,
in the daily choice to live awake,
in the countless moments to embrace
truth, love, presence.

The call never fades.
But now, you know its voice and how to answer.
You've braved the unknown — and found your way.
You've rewritten your story from within.
You've remembered your truth.

So rise.
Step forward.
Live with eyes wide open.
The world awaits —
and you, hero,
are only beginning.

Integrating the Journey: The Hero's Path as a Framework for Growth

As we near the close of this mythical journey
and perhaps a season of your own transformation —
pause to gaze back at the road you've traveled,
to see it anew,
with eyes that hold a deeper truth.

The Hero's Journey is not just a mythic tale,
nor a mere storytelling device
designed for amusement.
It's a living compass for inner growth,
a timeless framework that echoes across cultures,
resonating the pulse of real transformation —
the doubts you've wrestled,

the choices you've carved,
the strength you've summoned.

Through this lens, your life takes on new contours.
Not a rigid script,
but a rhythm shared by all who dare to grow:
Challenge. Descent. Revelation. Return.

The Hero's Journey isn't fantasy —
it's a map for authentic change,
a guide tracing how your growth unfolds,
not in neat steps, but in spirals,
in layers fused through struggle,
where clarity blooms after trial,
and wisdom rises from facing the darkness.

In challenge, you stretch.
In descent, you unearth your truest self.
In return, you weave what you've learned
into the very fabric of your life.

This is the path of transformation —
alive, untidy, and profoundly yours.

Crisis as the Catalyst for Transformation

Every challenge holds a spark of change —
a quiet call to grow,
even when the world seems to crumble around you.

The abyss — that moment of collapse —
is often the gateway to something profound,
a depth unreachable without first braving the chaos.

In that unraveling, clarity emerges —
not from the absence of turmoil,
but from learning to breathe within it,
letting the storm teach you
what calm never could.

Strength is born in the struggle,
not through sheer will,
but through the steady resolve
of a spirit that holds fast.

It's in the breaking that you find your true resilience,
the part of you that rises
when rising feels beyond reach

Transformation doesn't happen despite crisis —
it happens because of it,
through the dismantling of the self you once knew,
and the slow, powerful rebuilding
of something truer,
something more aligned
with your soul's deepest purpose.

Crisis isn't the opposite of growth.
It's the crucible where you are remade,
born anew in the raging fire.

You Are the Hero of Your Own Story

You are not a side character.
Not an extra in someone else's arc.
This is your story — yours alone.

The call finds you
in the spaces between certainty,
soft as a whisper
beneath life's steady hum.

Sometimes it arrives as crisis,
sometimes as quiet longing —
a restless ache that grows
until you can no longer ignore
the truth it carries.

You feel the pull — a spark stirring in depths
you'd forgotten you possessed,
beckoning you toward something
vast, raw, undeniably real.
Toward a life more alive,
more authentically yours
than any you've dared to imagine.

You face the trials, not as a bystander,
but as an active participant,
choosing to step forward — into uncertainty,
past towering obstacles,
through doubts that claim you're not enough.

You uncover truths meant only for you,
revelations that touch the edges of your being,
shaping who you are
and who you're still becoming.

These truths don't just transform you —
they ripple outward,
affecting the world through the way you live.

You don't become a hero by claiming victory.
No crown, no trophies,
no external prizes define you.
You become a hero
the moment you choose to walk the path,
the instant you answer the call,
stepping into your life with eyes wide open,
focused and fully awake to what lies ahead.

The hero isn't the one who never falters.
The hero is the one who keeps moving,
even when the way is steep,
even when shadows loom large.

And the truth is clear:
You've already begun your own journey.
You've chosen to walk this path.

Every step you take now,
carves you closer to the hero
you were always destined to be.

Growth Is Cyclical

The Hero's Journey isn't a singular act.
It's a spiral —
a living rhythm that weaves through your life,
A cycle of growth that never pauses.

You'll trace this path again —
in your bonds, your work, your inner world.

Each ending brings a fresh dawn,
every chapter's close unveils another,
each descent a deeper dive into the unknown,
an invitation to shed what's worn
and embrace what's waiting to bloom.

With every return, your insight deepens —
not just in facts,
but in the quiet knowing of your soul.
Each reentry roots you firmer
in the self you're becoming,
more connected to the truth of your journey.

You carry more with each cycle —
greater strength, sharper clarity, more awareness,
pieces of your soul that were once hidden,
now brought into the light.

This journey doesn't just push you forward —
it draws you inward,

anchoring you closer to your core,
until you stand as the self you've always been,
more fully claimed than ever before.

As this chapter fades,
the framework endures —
not to bind you,
but to light your way through the next spiral,
a reminder: the journey doesn't end —
It evolves.

You see it now:
You're not merely living a life.
You're weaving a story —
layered, expanding, shaped by your courage,
your growth,
your heart's desire to be more.
More not only for you,
but for those around you.

You get to shape how your story is told.
Every word, every turn, every choice
is yours to craft.

The Purpose of the Path

Understanding the Hero's Journey
as a model for personal growth
offers more than just insight —

it provides orientation.
A beacon through the fog,
a steady hand when life feels scattered or elusive.

In moments of doubt, when the path seems unclear,
you can pause and reflect:
Where do I stand on this journey?
What is this moment trying to teach me?
Who is it calling me to become?

This framework doesn't erase the sting of struggle
or pain —
it gives it form,
a place within the arc of your growth,
revealing meaning woven into the hardship.

It doesn't sidestep the chaos —
it guides you to find clarity within it,
showing that even in the tangle,
there's an order to be found.

The darkest moments no longer feel random.
They become logical parts of the story,
threads stitched into the vibrant tapestry of your life.

Your triumphs grow more precious —
not for their achievement,
but for the courage they demanded,
earned through the weight of your journey.

And the setbacks —
once seen as dead ends,
obstacles too vast to conquer —
unveil themselves as hidden gateways,
imploring you toward something greater.

When you feel lost — adrift in the heart of the night,
the path obscured,
wondering where it leads —
hold this truth:

You are not broken.
You are being recast.

This road you tread —
with its questions, its ache, its beauty, its growth —
this is the journey.

And you are the hero.
Not someday.
Not when you're healed, whole or certain.
Not when the world finally sees you.
But now.

Right now —
in the thick of uncertainty,
in the quiet weight of doubt,
you are already the hero.
Always.

Walking as the Hero

There will be days
when the journey slips from your grasp,
when the weight of the world presses harder
than the truth you've claimed.
When you wonder if your transformation was real —
or just a flicker in the dark,
a momentary spark that quickly fades.

But in the quiet stillness or in life's turmoils,
you'll remember:
The strength you forged wasn't fleeting or borrowed.
It was built — in raging fire, in stoic silence,
in unconditional love and complete surrender.
It pulses within you,
subtle yet unyielding,
woven into every step you now take.

You've crossed thresholds others dared not face,
embraced the unknown,
moved forward when the path lay hidden.

You've met your truest self —
not the polished facade,
but the raw, unfiltered you,
the one you were taught to hide.
And yet, you stayed. You endured.

That is heroism.
Not the absence of fear or doubt,
but the resolve to walk through it,
to climb when the path steepens,
to press on when the night stretches long.

No applause echoes at 5:00 a.m.,
only the soft rebellion of your alarm
against the world's permission to sleep.

Nobody counts the lonely nights
when discipline becomes your only companion,
the skipped parties that live on without you,
the quiet tears that salt your pillow
while dreams reshape themselves
into something harder, truer.

They don't witness the weight
of choosing yourself over comfort,
the daily deaths of who you used to be —
only the resurrection they call success,
the harvest they mistake for chance,
the strength they never saw you building
in the dark.

But here's the truth:
That's what makes it sacred.
That's what sets you apart.

Keep showing up when nobody's watching.
Keep building when no one believes.
Because the day you succeed,
they'll call it luck,
but you'll know better.

As this chapter draws to a close,
don't wait for life to deem you ready.
Don't seek the world's recognition
to affirm your growth.
You know who you are now —
and that is enough.

Step forward, walk on —
not because the way is certain,
but because you've become someone
who marches on regardless
of where the road takes you,
someone who knows
the journey itself is the destination.

Live with presence.
Lead with humility.
Carry your journey not as a burden —
but as a torch,
guiding those who follow,
the measure of all you've overcome,
and all you're still becoming.

The path will rise to meet you.
Though the horizon shimmers far,
it lies within your reach.
Your story —
luminous and precious,
still unfolding —
has only just begun.

And when doubt whispers that you've strayed too far,
remember:
you've already proven you can find your way back.

The Hero's Journey never truly ends —
it spirals upward,
each return preparing you
for depths you haven't yet imagined,
for versions of yourself still waiting in the dark,
ready to be called home.

You are one decision away
from a life-changing transformation.
There is a moment,
a flicker in time,
when everything changes.
It doesn't come with thunder.
It doesn't come with applause.

It comes in silence —
in the privacy of your own mind —
when you decide once and for all
that you will no longer be ruled
by fear,
by excuses,
by the life that was handed to you
instead of the one
you were born to build.

You are one decision away.
One decision from drawing a line in the sand
and saying,
No more waiting.
No more wishing.
No more blaming the world,
the economy,
your past,
your pain.

Because everything you need
is already within you,
and it always has been.
But until now,
it was dormant,
buried under layers of doubt,
distraction,
and disillusion.

But now you see it.
Now you feel it.
That electric pull in your chest,
the whisper that says,
It's time.

That whisper is destiny.
And destiny doesn't shout.
It waits.
It waits for you to rise.
It waits for you to choose.

Thomas Edison made over 1,000 attempts
before the light bulb blazed.
Not failures — attempts.
Every one a decision.
Every one a step closer to brilliance.

What would have happened
if he stopped at 999?
That's the difference between the ordinary
and the exceptional:
one more try,
one more refusal to quit,
one more decision to move forward
when everything inside you says
sit down and give up.

This is the truth
they don't teach in school,
the wisdom you won't find
in the noise of the world.

What Doesn't Break You

When I think of those
who have been through the worst —
through the dread that love lives with,
the kind that hollows out your chest
and leaves you gasping in the dark,
through the terrible fear
that anxiety can only dream of,
the paralysis that stops your breath
and makes each heartbeat thunder
like a countdown to collapse —

I feel something close to pity
for the rest,
for those who had it as they'd hoped,
who crossed the frozen river of life
from one safe shore to the other,
never guessing,
never sensing,
never knowing
the great dark churning beneath,
the depths that waited
with patient, ancient hunger.

But those for whom
the frozen river cracks and opens,
who fall through its brittle surface
into silent night —
not gradually,
not with warning,
but suddenly,
catastrophically —
while walking upright
in the ordinary light of this world,
believing themselves safe,
believing the ice would hold.

Whose hearts burst open
like fruit split by frost
and meet those freezing waters
with terrible intimacy,
who touch the bottom
of what it means to be alive
and mortal
and alone —
for them there is no consolation,
no words that reach that depth,
no comfort equal to their knowing.

Nor is there any need.
For they have seen what lies beneath
the surface of all things.
They have drowned and somehow breathed.
They have died and still are here.

And there is a strange, fierce grace in that —
a light that lives in them,
quiet as a candle,
steady as a star,
that those who crossed on solid ice
will never know.

8

17 STEPS OF THE HERO'S JOURNEY

Here lies the map of your becoming —
seventeen steps that trace the arc
from who you are
to who you're called to be.

Each step a doorway,
each phase a teacher,
each movement forward a choice to trust
the ancient wisdom
that lives within your bones.
They are markers on the spiral path
that leads you home
to yourself.

For thousands of years,
this pattern has repeated —
in myths and legends,
in the quiet heroics of ordinary people
who dare to grow.

Not every journey follows this exact sequence,
but every authentic transformation
touches these all-important waypoints
on the path to wholeness.

DEPARTURE

1. The Call to Adventure

A spark ignites — a moment, a person,
a restless pull within.
Your familiar world shifts,
the ground beneath certainty suddenly unsteady.

Something interrupts the rhythm
of your ordinary days —
a crisis that cracks you open,
a longing that won't be silenced,
a challenge wrapped in invitation.

Not loud, but insistent,
it whispers of paths untaken,
of a self you've never met.

The call beckons you forward —
toward the unseen,
toward a truth that waits
just beyond the edge of everything you know.

2. Refusal of the Call

You hesitate,
feet planted at the threshold of everything familiar.
The known wraps around you —
worn edges, predictable contours,
a life that no longer fits
but still feels safer than the vast unknown.

Doubts stir like restless shadows:
Am I ready?
Can I face what waits ahead?
What if I'm not strong enough?
What if I lose myself in the trying?

Fear whispers its seductions —
Stay. Settle. Don't risk what little peace you have.
The comfort zone may feel small,
suffocating even,
but it asks nothing of you
that you haven't already given.

This reluctance is vital,
the heart's cautious dance with destiny.

For in this very resistance —
this questioning,
this trembling at the edge —
the seed of change takes root.
To doubt is human.
To question is to begin awakening.

3. Supernatural Aid

A guide appears —
not always grand,
but always exactly when you need them most.
A mentor with knowing eyes,
a friend who sees your potential,
a stranger bearing the precise words
your soul was waiting to hear.

They arrive carrying gifts —
tools for the journey ahead,
wisdom wrapped in story,
courage disguised as conversation.
Sometimes it's a book that falls open
to the page you needed,
a chance encounter that shifts everything,
or simply a presence that says without words:
You are not alone.

Their offering holds power —
not to carry your burden,
but to light the torch you'll carry forward.

They remind you of the strength you already hold,
the wisdom you've forgotten,
the hero you've always been
but were afraid to claim.

With their blessing,
you step boldly into the vast unknown,
equipped not just with tools,
but with the knowledge
that guidance flows to those brave enough to begin.

4. Crossing the Threshold

You choose.
The moment arrives when hesitation dissolves
into decisive action.
The boundary between worlds
shimmers before you —
known on one side, mystery on the other.

You step through.
Feel the shift beneath your feet —
solid ground giving way to untested terrain.
The air tastes different here,
charged with possibility
and electric with risk.

No turning back now.
The familiar world fades like a dream upon waking,
its safety and limitations are equally distant.

You've crossed the line
that separates who you were
from who you might become.

This is commitment incarnate —
embracing the path ahead with all its uncertainties,
its promise of trials that will test your mettle,
its whispered invitation to become more
than you ever dared imagine.
You are no longer a visitor
to your own transformation.
You are participant, protagonist,
pioneer of your own evolution.

5. Belly of the Whale

You plunge into the depths —
swallowed whole by the unfamiliar,
digested by darkness
that breathes with ancient knowing.
This is the belly of your rebirth,
a place where light struggles to reach,
where shadows whisper truths
you've spent years learning not to hear.

The unknown engulfs you like a living thing,
its walls pressing close,
testing not just resolve
but the very foundations
of who you believed yourself to be.

Here, in this pivotal dissolution,
you face what you've long avoided —
the parts of yourself
that frighten,
that shame,
that call for reckoning.

This is surrender — not defeat,
but the holy unraveling of an outgrown skin.
The old self begins its necessary breaking,
each crack a doorway to what waits beneath.
In this first forge of your metamorphosis,
you discover that sometimes you must be undone
before you can be remade.

INITIATION

6. The Road of Trials

The path grows rugged — no longer a gentle slope
but a jagged ascent
where each step demands everything you have
and more than you knew you possessed.

Trials arrive like storms — sudden, relentless,
each one designed to test a different layer
of your remaking.

Internal battles that rage in sleepless hours,
external forces that seem bent on your surrender,
emotional tempests that strip you bare
and leave you questioning
everything you thought you understood.

Some tests you pass.
Others break you open, teaching through failure
what success never could.
Each stumble carves deeper wisdom,
each victory builds muscles you didn't know
your spirit embodied.

The road strips away illusion after illusion —
who you thought you were,
what you believed you needed,
how you imagined strength would feel.
What remains is raw, real,
resilient beyond measure —
the unshakeable core that was always there,
waiting to be discovered,
claimed,
trusted.

7. The Meeting with the Goddess
A moment of grace arrives —
unexpected, luminous,
like sunlight breaking through storm clouds
you didn't realize had been gathering.

She appears —
not always in flesh, but in presence
that speaks to the deepest chambers of your heart.
Sometimes a person whose love asks nothing
yet offers everything,
sometimes the whisper of your own inner wisdom
finally loud enough to be heard.

This is unconditional love made manifest —
a force that sees not who you've been
or who you should become,
but who you are in this vulnerable moment,
flawed and striving
and utterly worthy of compassion.

Her presence awakens what you'd forgotten —
that you are not alone in this struggle,
that love is not earned but recognized,
that the wholeness you seek
was never really lost,
only covered by layers of forgetting.

This encounter becomes the ember you carry
through darker passages,
the vision that reminds you
what's worth fighting for —
not perfection,
but the courage
to love yourself through this remaking.

To tend the light
that burns within
even when winds howl
and the path grows cold.

8. Woman as Temptress

A lure emerges — seductive, glittering,
wearing the face of everything
you thought you wanted.
Not always love, but ease that whispers
you've suffered enough,
wealth that promises
this will solve everything,
fame that flatters
you deserve recognition.

The temptation knows your weaknesses,
speaks your secret language of unfulfilled desires.
It offers shortcuts to satisfaction,
detours that seem to lead toward happiness
but pull you sideways
from the path you've bled to walk.

This is the test of divided loyalty —
will you choose the immediate comfort
over the distant promise?
The familiar pleasure
over the unknown growth?

The flashy distraction
over the steady flame of purpose you've tended
through so much darkness?

To resist is to sharpen focus
like a blade against the whetstone of temptation.
To choose the truth you've claimed
over the seductive call of what feels easier,
safer, more immediately gratifying.
In this refusal,
your commitment becomes unshakeable,
your purpose refined to its essence.

9. Atonement with the Father

A shadow looms — massive, familiar,
bearing the weight
of every wound you've carried,
every voice that told you
you are not enough.

The father appears —
not always flesh and blood,
but the embodiment of authority that shaped you.
The limiting beliefs carved into your bones,
the inherited patterns that have ruled your choices
from the shadows of unconscious memory.

This is the confrontation you've avoided,
circled around,
made excuses to delay.
Face to face with the source of your deepest fears,
your most persistent doubts,
the very forces that convinced you
to stay small,
stay safe,
stay silent.

Here, in this sacred arena, you must choose:
Will you bow again to the old tyranny,
or will you stand in the truth of who you've become?
Forgiveness flows —
not as weakness,
but as the ultimate act of self-liberation.
You release their hold,
reconcile with the past,
or simply refuse to carry their judgment
one step further.

This reckoning cracks the foundation
of your former prison,
freeing you to walk with a purpose
no longer clouded by shadow,
your clarity born from the courage
to face what you once fled.

10. Apotheosis

Light breaks through — not gradual dawn,
but sudden illumination
that renders everything startlingly clear.
The veils fall away,
and you see your own vastness —
not as arrogance, but as recognition
of what was always true.

This is awakening beyond mere understanding —
a cellular shift where wisdom enters
not only through the mind
but through every fiber of your being.
You feel your connection
to the infinite web that holds all things.
Your place in the cosmos no longer questioned
but deeply known.

The old self —
with its limitations,
its fears,
its careful boundaries —
dissolves like mist before the rising sun.
What remains is essence purified,
power integrated,
purpose crystallized
into unshakeable knowing.

You stand transformed —
not perfect, but whole,
equipped with wisdom
forged in the crucible of your own becoming.
Ready now to face the journey's fiercest trials
not with bravado,
but with the quiet certainty of one who has touched
the source of their own unlimited strength.

11. The Ultimate Boon

You reach the center —
the heart of all you've fought to claim.
Here lies the prize, not glittering gold
or fleeting glory,
but something far more precious:
the truth you came to find,
the freedom you bled to earn,
the insight that transforms
everything you thought you knew about yourself.

This is the boon
beyond all imagination —
earned not through luck
but through the currency of courage,
paid for with pieces of who you used to be,
purchased with the willingness
to walk through fire
and emerge fundamentally changed.

It fills your hands, this treasure —
weightless yet immense,
simple yet revolutionary.
You understand now why the journey demanded
everything of you:
only by losing yourself completely
could you find what was always yours to claim.

Yet even in this moment of triumphant arrival,
you sense the deeper truth:
the quest is not complete.
The boon in your hands carries responsibility —
to return,
to share,
to let this gift ripple outward
into a world that waits
for what you've learned to give.

RETURN

12. Refusal of the Return
The world calls you back —
that familiar place with its old expectations,
its unchanged rhythms,
its people who still see you as who you used to be.

But your heart resists, clinging to this new sanctuary
where everything makes sense,
where your evolution feels safe,
protected, real.

The new self you've claimed feels too vast,
too tender,
too precious
for the smallness you once called home.

Here, truth flows like clear water.
Here, your purpose burns bright
without question.
Why return to a world that might diminish this light,
doubt your change,
pressure you to shrink back into shapes
you've already outgrown?

The temptation whispers:
Stay. Rest. Guard what you've gained.
Let others find their own way to this clarity.

Yet something deeper stirs beneath the fear —
the understanding
that true growth cannot hide in isolation,
that wisdom hoarded becomes stagnant,
that the boon you've claimed
was never meant for you alone.

The return demands courage of a different kind:
not just to venture forth, but to bring forth
the light you've found
into a world that needs it
more than you know.

13. The Magic Flight

You move toward home —
the boon clutched close,
precious cargo that pulses with power
you're still learning to understand.

But the path betrays you with one last gauntlet,
as if the universe itself conspires to test
whether you truly deserve
what you've claimed.

Obstacles materialize from thin air —
final guardians
that rise to challenge your worthiness.
Shadows give chase,
whispering doubts:
You're not ready.
You'll lose it all.
Turn back while you can.

The weight of the treasure
grows heavier with each step,
not in mass
but in responsibility.
Do you understand what you carry?
Can you protect it from those who would
steal, corrupt, or diminish its power?

This flight becomes the crucible
that burns away
any remaining doubt about your readiness.
Each obstacle overcome
proves you worthy of the gift you bear.
Your resolve sharpens
like a blade tested in fire,
ensuring your truth will not only endure
but blaze bright
through whatever the return demands.

14. Rescue from Without

A hand reaches out —
unexpected, perfectly timed,
just when the strain of carrying your treasure
threatens to overwhelm your weary spirit.
A friend who sees your struggle,
a guide who remembers their own return,
a moment of grace
that arrives disguised as ordinary kindness.

They don't offer to bear your load —
the boon is yours to carry,
yours to protect,
yours to integrate.
But they steady your trembling steps,
offer water for the parched journey,
share the wisdom of their own crossing
between worlds.

This rescue reminds you
of what the solitary trials made you forget:
transformation may begin in isolation,
but it completes itself in connection.
You were never meant to walk this path
entirely alone.
Never destined to shoulder
the full weight of your journey without support.

Their presence becomes a bridge
between the world you're leaving
and the one you're entering —
helping you carry not just the treasure,
but the courage to trust
that others will understand
the gift you bring.

15. The Crossing of the Return Threshold

You step back into your old ordinary world —
same streets,
same faces,
same rhythms in familiar spaces
that once defined the boundaries
of your once-cherished home turf.
But you are forever changed,
carrying within you a fire that burns
with different light.

The challenge unfolds
not in grand gestures
but in countless small moments:
How do you speak your newfound truth
to ears that expect the old you?
How do you honor the wisdom earned
in sacred spaces
while navigating
grocery stores and morning commutes?

Old patterns rise like familiar ghosts,
whispering seductions:
Slip back. It's easier.
No one will notice if you pretend nothing's changed.
But your bones remember the fire,
your heart knows the weight of the boon
you now carry.

This crossing demands a different kind of courage:
not the boldness to venture forth,
but the persistence to weave your truth
into the fabric of ordinary days.
To stand firm in who you've become
even when the world still calls you
by your former name.

16. Master of Two Worlds
Balance takes root —
not the fragile equilibrium
of carefully held opposites,
but the fluid grace of integration,
where the self you've crafted
through ordeal and revelation
dances seamlessly with the world
you've returned to embrace.

You move freely between both realms —
one foot planted in the hallowed ground
of your awakening,
the other stepping confidently
through the everyday demands of ordinary life.
No longer torn between who you were
and who you've become,
but whole,
complete,
at peace with the beautiful complexity
of being fully human.

This is the wisdom of the bridge-builder:
to honor your growth
without abandoning the practical world,
to carry your truth
without preaching,
to embody your insights
without losing touch
with the ground beneath your feet.

You've become a living testament
to the possibility of profound change —
walking proof that one can dive deep
into the mysteries of their complex self
and still return in time to make dinner,
pay bills,
love fiercely
in the midst of the beautifully
ordinary world.

17. Freedom to Live
You stand unbound —
not free from challenge, but free within it,
no longer captive
to the voices that once whispered limitations
into your willing ears.
The past holds no chains,
the future no terrors you cannot meet
with a steady heart.

This is freedom
earned through descent,
paid for with courage,
blessed by the willingness to become
what you were afraid to even imagine.

You live now with authenticity as your compass,
embodying each lesson not as burden
but as gift,

walking proof that transformation
is not only possible
but inevitable
for those brave enough to answer the call.

Your light becomes a beacon
for others still lost in the maze
of their own metamorphosis.
Your presence a whisper:
The journey is real.
The destination is you.

Ever-evolving, ever-deepening.
You step into each new chapter
not as one seeking
but as one who has learned to trust the path
that unfolds beneath willing feet.

This is the Hero's Journey —
not ancient myth
but living map,
not distant story
but your own transcendence,
guiding each step,
each spiral toward the self
you were always destined to become.

≈

The Hero's Journey in Cinema

Hollywood has embraced the *monomyth* (the common heroic narrative in which a heroic protagonist sets out, has transformative adventures, and returns home) in many different ways. These are three of the most popular films that explore the hero's journey, broken down into the main stages of the monomyth.

Star Wars (1977)

1. The Ordinary World

Luke Skywalker lives a simple, unremarkable life on the desert planet Tatooine, working on his uncle's moisture farm. He spends his days staring at the twin suns setting on the horizon, dreaming of adventure and escape from the monotony of his world. His life is familiar, predictable, and steeped in isolation — yet there's a restlessness within him, a yearning for something more. He's ready for change, even if he doesn't know it yet.

2. The Call to Adventure

The call comes in the form of a distress message from Princess Leia, hidden inside the droid R2-D2. The message asks for help to transport the droid to Alderaan, a mission that holds great importance to the Rebellion. It's an unexpected interruption in Luke's mundane life, but it stirs something deep within him — a connection to a greater purpose.

Though he's reluctant, something in his heart knows that this is the beginning of a life he's always longed for.

3. Refusal of the Call

At first, Luke resists the call to adventure. He's tied to his family and his life on Tatooine. When Obi-Wan Kenobi tells him about the greater forces at play, Luke hesitates. He's unsure, not fully understanding the consequences of this new journey. He doubts himself and is wary of leaving the security of home, especially after his uncle discourages him from pursuing such a dangerous path. Luke's initial refusal is grounded in his fear of the unknown and his sense of responsibility to his old life.

4. The Mentor

Obi-Wan Kenobi enters the story as a guide and mentor, encouraging Luke to embrace his destiny. He reveals the truth about Luke's father, showing him the lightsaber — a symbol of his legacy as a Jedi Knight. Obi-Wan teaches Luke about the Force, the power that binds all living things together. Through Obi-Wan's wisdom and faith in him, Luke begins to see that the life he was meant for is far greater than he ever imagined. Obi-Wan's mentorship stirs something deep within Luke, awakening the hero in him.

5. Crossing the Threshold

Luke finally decides to leave Tatooine, crossing the

threshold into the unknown when he and Obi-Wan travel to Mos Eisley. This moment signifies Luke's commitment to the journey ahead. It's a literal and figurative departure from his old life, leaving the safety of Tatooine and entering a wider, more dangerous galaxy. He's now fully committed to his quest, even though he's unsure of what lies ahead.

6. The Ordeal

Luke's first true test comes when he and his allies attempt to rescue Princess Leia from the clutches of the Empire aboard the Death Star. The action-packed sequence of rescuing Leia from captivity is just the beginning of Luke's transformation. But the greatest test comes when Luke, with the help of the Force, destroys the Death Star in a daring attack. This victory is pivotal — it shows that Luke is more than just a farm boy. He's developing the courage, skills, and belief in himself to become a hero. The ordeal also marks his first real encounter with the immense power of the Force and sets the stage for his growth as a Jedi.

7. The Return

Having completed his mission, Luke returns to the Rebellion, not as the uncertain young man who left Tatooine, but as someone who has tasted both victory and loss. His decision to continue on the path of the Jedi is clear. He joins the Rebel Alliance, solidifying his commitment to fight against the Empire. Luke's return isn't just physical; it's a return to his true self, the beginning of his journey as a Jedi and a hero.

The struggles he faced have shaped him into someone ready for greater challenges and deeper responsibilities. Luke's transformation is just beginning, and this return marks the start of a new chapter in his hero's journey.

The Matrix (1999)

1. The Ordinary World

Thomas Anderson, also known by his hacker alias *Neo*, lives a double life. By day, he's a bored and disillusioned computer programmer working in a soulless corporate job. By night, he's immersed in the underground world of hacking, searching for something that doesn't quite exist — answers to questions he's not fully aware of. His existence is defined by confusion, a sense of being trapped in a system he doesn't fully understand. Neo's world is ordinary, yet the cracks in it are beginning to show. He feels a pull, an unspoken desire for something more, though he can't name it yet.

2. The Call to Adventure

The call comes when Neo is contacted by a group of rebels, led by Morpheus, who promises him the truth. Neo receives a cryptic message urging him to "follow the white rabbit," which leads him to a life-altering encounter with Trinity. She shows him that everything he believes about the world is a lie. The "call" is not only external, but deeply personal — it's the awakening to a truth that Neo can't deny, even though it threatens to shatter everything he thought he knew.

3. Refusal of the Call

Initially, Neo resists the call to adventure. He's skeptical and afraid of what this new truth might mean for his life. Morpheus and Trinity offer him a choice: to stay in the familiar, comfortable world, or to step into the unknown and face reality as it truly is. Neo hesitates, and for a time, allows himself to be captured, unsure whether he can trust what is being presented to him. The **Refusal of the Call** is an inner conflict between the desire for truth and the fear of losing the illusion of control and security.

4. The Mentor

Morpheus enters as Neo's mentor, offering him a choice that will change his life forever: the blue pill, which will allow him to continue living in the illusion, or the red pill, which will reveal the truth about the Matrix. Morpheus is a guide, showing Neo the path to self-realization and the ultimate truth. Morpheus represents the mentor archetype, pushing Neo to embrace his destiny and his potential. The mentor doesn't force Neo to take the red pill, but he offers the opportunity to see the world through new eyes — to choose his own path, knowing the choice itself transforms everything.

5. Crossing the Threshold

Neo makes the choice. He swallows the red pill, and his journey begins. This moment is the **Crossing of the Threshold**, a symbolic entry into the unknown. He is shown the truth about the Matrix — the world he's known is nothing but a simulated reality, designed to keep humanity enslaved while machines harvest their energy. The real world, the one Neo has been blind to, is dark and dystopian, but it is where the truth lies. This moment signifies a complete break from his old life, an irreversible choice that marks the beginning of his transformation.

6. The Ordeal

As Neo struggles to accept his new reality, he is thrown into intense trials. The **Ordeal** is Neo's struggle with accepting his new identity as "The One," the person destined to free humanity from the Matrix. It's a difficult journey filled with self-doubt and resistance. He faces Agent Smith, the embodiment of the Matrix's controlling forces, and in a pivotal moment, Neo learns to trust in the Force, his inner strength, and the knowledge that he is capable of far more than he thought. By the end of the ordeal, he defeats Agent Smith and saves Morpheus, symbolizing the power of self-realization and acceptance.

7. The Return

The final step in Neo's transformation is **The Return.** As

Neo stands in the heart of the Matrix, now fully aware of his power, he declares that he will defeat the machines and free humanity. His return is not just physical but spiritual. Neo understands that his true purpose is to live out the truth he's discovered, to act with clarity, strength, and purpose. He embraces the responsibility of his new identity as "The One," a symbol of hope for humanity. The journey is far from over, but Neo has stepped into his true power, and he's ready to reshape the world in his image. His return signifies the beginning of his mission, and with it, the evolution of his purpose.

The Lord of the Rings: The Fellowship of the Ring (2001)

1. The Ordinary World

Frodo Baggins lives a peaceful, idyllic life in the Shire, a quiet, rural region in Middle-earth. He's content, perhaps even a bit complacent, in his simple existence. He has little desire for adventure or conflict. His world is defined by the small comforts of home, the love of his uncle Bilbo, and the familiarity of the Shire's green hills. He is, in many ways, unaware of the greater forces at play in the world, living in a state of blissful ignorance.

2. The Call to Adventure

The call to adventure comes unexpectedly when Frodo inherits the One Ring from his uncle Bilbo. The Ring, a symbol of great power and malice, is central to the survival of

Middle-earth, but Frodo is unaware of its true danger at first. When Gandalf reveals the Ring's dark history and its potential to destroy the world, Frodo is thrust into a conflict far greater than anything he could have imagined. The call to adventure is not just an external event, but a deeper pull within Frodo — a realization that his life will never be the same again.

3. Refusal of the Call

Frodo is initially reluctant to leave the comfort of the Shire and take on such a heavy responsibility. He's afraid, unsure of his own capabilities, and reluctant to leave his peaceful life behind. The **Refusal of the Call** is seen in his hesitation and desire to keep the Ring in the Shire, where he believes it's safe. He fears the journey's dangers and doubts his ability to fulfill this monumental task. This stage reflects the **unwillingness** to face what lies beyond the known and the comfort of the familiar.

4. The Mentor

Gandalf serves as Frodo's mentor, providing guidance, wisdom, and protection. He leads Frodo into understanding the weight of the Ring and the responsibility it carries. Gandalf doesn't take the journey for Frodo, but instead shows him the path, offering insight into the history of the Ring and the forces at work in Middle-earth. Gandalf's role is pivotal in guiding Frodo to trust in himself and the importance of his mission.

5. Crossing the Threshold

Frodo crosses the threshold when he leaves the Shire with the Ring, leaving behind his quiet life and entering the wider world. He is joined by a fellowship of companions, each with their own skills and strengths. This step marks the **point of no return**, where Frodo fully commits to his role in the battle against Sauron. The familiar world of the Shire is left behind, and Frodo steps into the unknown, fully aware that he may never return.

6. The Ordeal

The first major **ordeal** comes in the form of the many trials Frodo faces on the journey to Rivendell. The pursuit by the Ringwraiths, the dangers of the wilderness, and the internal doubts and fears that arise all push Frodo's limits. The external threats — especially from the Ringwraiths — force Frodo to act with greater courage than he thought possible. His internal trial is about accepting his own strength and destiny. The ordeal helps Frodo face the reality of the journey he's undertaken and prepares him for the greater trials ahead.

7. The Meeting with the Goddess

This stage may not be as overt in *The Lord of the Rings*, but Frodo's meeting with **Galadriel**, the Lady of Lothlórien, plays a key role in his transformation. Galadriel, a powerful and wise figure, offers Frodo counsel, gifts, and a moment of clarity. She reflects back to him the potential of his path, and shows him a vision of what could happen if he fails. Her presence is deeply comforting and reassuring, helping Frodo understand that his journey is part of something much greater than himself.

8. Woman as Temptress

Frodo's temptation to stray from the quest is most evident when the Ring begins to exert its pull over him. The **temptation** of the Ring, especially as Frodo realizes its power, calls him to abandon the mission and keep the Ring for himself. This is not a conventional love interest temptation, but the Ring itself acts as the "temptress," trying to seduce Frodo into using its power for personal gain. The temptation represents Frodo's **inner conflict** between good and evil, his struggle to resist the Ring's allure.

9. Atonement with the Father

The **atonement** occurs when Frodo faces the reality of the burden he carries, especially after Boromir's attempt to take the Ring from him. Boromir's betrayal and the breaking of the fellowship force Frodo to confront the consequences of his journey and the weight of his responsibility. He must reconcile with the harsh truth that the world is not as simple as he thought and that the Ring's power can corrupt even the best of intentions. It's a powerful moment of realization and self-awareness.

10. Apotheosis

In the wake of the fellowship's division, Frodo's **apotheosis** occurs when he decides to continue the journey alone with Sam, knowing that the Ring's power is too great to risk it being taken by others. Frodo's understanding of his purpose deepens. He realizes that the journey is not just about destroying the Ring — it's about **embracing his role as a bearer of hope**, even when that hope seems fleeting. This realization prepares him for the hardest part of his journey — facing his deepest fears and doubts.

11. The Ultimate Boon

The **ultimate boon** is the moment when Frodo reaches Mount Doom and is ready to destroy the Ring. This is the climax of his journey — the culmination of everything he's endured. It's not just the physical act of destroying the Ring, but the inner victory of overcoming the **temptation** to claim the Ring for himself. Frodo doesn't succeed in the way he intended, but the Ring is destroyed through Gollum's actions, signaling that the **boon** — the salvation of Middle-earth — has been achieved through selflessness and sacrifice.

The Hero's Journey in Literature

Many authors have used the monomyth in literature and popular fiction. Let's explore the hero's journey in *The Alchemist* and *Harry Potter* — two famous epics:

Paulo Coelho, *The Alchemist* (1988)

1. The Ordinary World

Santiago, a young shepherd, lives in the fields of Andalusia, Spain. His life is simple, filled with the peaceful routine of tending to his sheep. Though content, Santiago has a deep yearning for something more. He dreams of a treasure buried near the Egyptian pyramids and is haunted by the sense that his life is meant for greater things. His world, though calm and secure, feels too small for his growing curiosity and desire for adventure.

2. The Call to Adventure

Santiago's call to adventure comes in the form of a recurring dream. In it, he is told that a treasure is waiting for him at the base of the Egyptian pyramids. This dream becomes an unshakable feeling that compels him to leave the comfort of his life as a shepherd. He meets a gypsy fortune-teller who encourages him to pursue this treasure, reinforcing the call to step into the unknown and seek his Personal Legend.

3. Refusal of the Call

At first, Santiago hesitates to leave his life behind. He's unsure of the treasure's existence and doubts whether he should abandon his sheep, his simple life, and the familiar world he knows. He wrestles with fear, uncertainty, and the attachment to comfort. The refusal is natural — he doesn't want to take a risk on something so uncertain. But his yearning for purpose, for deeper meaning, is too strong to ignore for long.

4. The Mentor

Santiago meets Melchizedek, the King of Salem, who becomes his mentor. Melchizedek introduces Santiago to the concept of the *Personal Legend* — the unique path that each person must follow to realize their fullest potential. The king gives Santiago two stones, Urim and Thummim, to help him make decisions along the way, and imparts wisdom about following omens. Melchizedek's role is to push Santiago to trust in his quest, encouraging him to pursue the treasure and reminding him that the journey itself is part of the treasure.

5. Crossing the Threshold

Santiago finally decides to leave his home and embark on the journey to find his treasure. He crosses the threshold when he sells his sheep and sets out for Tangier, Morocco, in search of the treasure he believes is waiting for him. This moment marks the beginning of his adventure into the unknown. He's leaving behind everything he knows — his home, his comfort, and his predictable life — to seek something greater. There is no turning back now; the path forward is his only choice.

6. The Ordeal

Once in Tangier, Santiago faces a number of trials. He is swindled out of his money by a man who promises to help him find his treasure. This experience leaves him with nothing, forcing him to start over in a foreign land. Santiago is tested not only by external challenges but also by his internal doubts and fears. He has to summon the courage to continue when it feels like the world is conspiring against him. His ordeal teaches him the importance of resilience and learning from mistakes.

7. The Meeting with the Goddess

Santiago's meeting with the **goddess** occurs when he meets **Fatima**, a woman at an oasis. She represents love, but also spiritual wisdom. Their meeting helps Santiago realize that love is part of his journey — it isn't something that takes him away from his purpose but is instead a part of his transformation. Fatima symbolizes Santiago's connection to the soul of the world, teaching him that love is a driving force, both in following his Personal Legend and in living fully.

8. Woman as Temptress

Santiago faces the **temptation** to stay at the oasis with Fatima, torn between his love for her and his quest to find the treasure. This represents a significant inner conflict, as Santiago must choose between the world of love and comfort, and the pursuit of his deeper purpose. The temptation to stay with Fatima challenges him to confront his fear of loss and his desire for a simpler, safer life. But Santiago realizes that to fully embrace love, he must first fulfill his own destiny.

9. Atonement with the Father

Santiago's **atonement** with his metaphorical "father" comes when he faces the reality of his quest and his relationship with his dreams. In the desert, Santiago has a vision that connects him to the soul of the world. In this vision, he confronts both his fears and his hopes, coming to terms with the deep responsibility he has to fulfill his Personal Legend. The vision is a moment of reconciliation — Santiago realizes that the treasure is not just material, but is about the wisdom and growth he's gained through the journey.

10. Apotheosis

Santiago's **apotheosis** occurs when he learns to interpret the language of the world, understanding that the universe conspires to help those who pursue their Personal Legend. He gains a profound sense of his place in the world, feeling at one with it. Santiago's transformation is complete as he achieves a deeper understanding of life and his connection to it. He now sees the world and his journey through the lens of spiritual insight, understanding that the treasure he seeks is a metaphor for the wisdom and experiences he's gained.

ii. The Ultimate Boon

The **ultimate boon** arrives when Santiago finally reaches the Egyptian pyramids and unearths his treasure. However, the true boon is not in the material wealth he finds, but in the realization that the journey itself — the trials, the lessons, and the connections he made — was the true treasure. Santiago's growth, his understanding of the world, and his connection to the soul of the world are the rewards of his quest. He realizes that the treasure was always within him — it was his personal transformation, his wisdom, and his ability to see the world with new eyes.

J.K. Rowling, *Harry Potter and the Sorcerer's Stone* (1997)

i. The Ordinary World

Harry Potter's life begins in the world of the ordinary — or rather, the *unordinary*. He lives with his cruel aunt and uncle, Vernon and Petunia Dursley, in a small cupboard under the stairs. Harry is mistreated, neglected, and told that his parents died in a car crash. The truth about his magical heritage is hidden from him, and he grows up with feelings of inadequacy, confusion, and isolation. His world is mundane, yet he carries a strange sense of not truly belonging, as though something extraordinary is waiting to be revealed. That feeling, however faint, refuses to leave him—a persistent whisper that his life is meant to be more than this small, suffocating existence.

2. The Call to Adventure

The call to adventure comes in the form of a mysterious letter — an invitation to attend Hogwarts School of Witchcraft and Wizardry. This letter is the first of many that disrupt Harry's ordinary life. Despite the best efforts of the Dursleys to prevent it, Harry learns that he is not ordinary at all. He's a wizard, and the world of magic has been waiting for him. The letter, and the subsequent arrival of Hagrid, who physically brings Harry to Hogwarts, is an undeniable sign that his life is about to change.

3. Refusal of the Call

Harry, at first, is skeptical. He doesn't understand what's happening, and when confronted with the reality of being a wizard, it's overwhelming. How could he be a wizard? He had always been told he was nothing special. The mystery surrounding his parents' death also complicates matters — Harry doesn't know the truth about his parents' magical legacy and the evil wizard who killed them. The **Refusal of the Call** is Harry's initial disbelief — his difficulty accepting the truth about who he really is.

4. The Mentor

Hagrid, a giant of a man and a kind-hearted magical being, serves as Harry's first true mentor. Hagrid not only introduces Harry to the magical world but also begins to teach him about his own identity as a wizard. Hagrid takes Harry to Diagon Alley, buys him all his magical supplies, and explains the basics of what it means to be a wizard. Hagrid is patient and loyal, but it's really the guidance of **Albus Dumbledore**, the wise headmaster of Hogwarts, that helps Harry understand his true purpose. Both Hagrid and Dumbledore offer Harry wisdom, protection, and the opportunity to understand his journey as a hero.

5. Crossing the Threshold

The **Crossing of the Threshold** occurs when Harry steps through the magical barrier at King's Cross Station and boards the Hogwarts Express. As he crosses the magical barrier onto Platform 9 ¾, he enters a world entirely unlike his own — a world of magic, wonder, and unimaginable possibility. This moment symbolizes his departure from his old life and his entry into a new, unknown realm, where the adventure will truly begin. It's a literal and symbolic crossing from ordinary life into the extraordinary.

6. The Ordeal

Harry faces numerous challenges and tests during his first year at Hogwarts. The **Ordeal** includes the challenges of fitting in, learning magic, and making new friends. But the greatest trial comes when Harry uncovers the secret of the Philosopher's Stone — the magical object that Voldemort seeks to regain his power. Harry must confront the dangers of the dark forces at Hogwarts, including encounters with the deadly Devil's Snare, the chess game of life and death, and, ultimately, a direct confrontation with Voldemort's spirit. In the climax of the book, Harry, using courage and quick thinking, defeats Voldemort's possession of Professor Quirrell and protects the Stone, marking the moment he stands up to the darkness and proves his bravery.

7. The Return

After the intense experiences at Hogwarts, Harry returns to the Dursleys for the summer, as he must each year. But now, he is forever changed. He is not the same boy who was locked away in a cupboard. He knows who he is, and the wizarding world, with its promises of adventure, friendship, and greatness, now calls to him. The **Return** is not just physical; it's a return to the ordinary world, but Harry now understands that his journey is far from over. He returns with a deeper understanding of his identity, his purpose, and the challenges that lie ahead. Though he is still young and unsure, he is no longer unaware of the significance of his life and the role he must play in the magical world.

Reflection Exercise: Mapping Your Heroic Journey

1. Think of a time in your life when you experienced significant change or growth. Identify the different stages of the Hero's Journey in that experience. What was your "call to adventure"?

Reflect on the moment or situation that pushed you out of your comfort zone, whether it was an external event, an internal urge, or a quiet shift in your perception. What inspired you to begin this journey? Was it a clear call, or did it come as a subtle nudge that you only noticed in hindsight? The *call* can be loud or quiet, obvious or hidden — but it always marks the beginning of your transformation.

2. Did you face any initial resistance or doubt? What was it that made you hesitate?

We often resist the call, whether because of fear, uncertainty, or a deep attachment to our old ways of being. The Hero's Journey is not just about stepping forward; it's also about the moment we realize we *must* change, despite our doubts. Reflect on the fears and insecurities that arose. Did you second-guess yourself? Were there moments when you thought about turning back? How did you overcome those feelings? Or are they still with you, in some form, today?

3. How did this experience change you? What wisdom or strength did you gain from it?

Transformation is not just about learning new skills or gaining knowledge; it's about a fundamental shift in who we are. The Hero's Journey brings us face-to-face with our vulnerabilities, fears, and strengths — and through that confrontation, we are reshaped. How has this experience altered your outlook on life? What wisdom have you gained that you now carry forward? Perhaps it's a greater sense of inner strength, a new understanding of your purpose, or a more profound connection with others. Consider the ways in which you have evolved and what qualities you've discovered or honed within yourself.

4. Write about this experience as if you were the hero of your own story.

Include key moments such as crossing the threshold, facing challenges, and returning with a new perspective.
When we view our experiences through the lens of the Hero's Journey, it allows us to reframe the struggles and triumphs in a more empowering light. Step into the story of your life and see yourself as the Hero. How did you cross the threshold from the ordinary to the extraordinary? What were the major obstacles or tests you faced, and how did you rise to meet them? Reflect on the transformation that occurred during your journey. Then, think about the return: how did you bring your newfound wisdom back into your life? How has this experience reshaped your perspective, your relationships, and your daily choices?

The Hero's Journey in Your Life

Having mapped your own heroic journey,
you now stand at the threshold
of a deeper understanding —
seeing your entire life
through this transformative lens.

Understanding the Hero's Journey
allows us to accept every challenge, every shift,
not as a random interruption,
but as essential chapters
in the story of our growth.

It's a blueprint for transformation.
A map of the soul —
reminding us that each trial, every obstacle,
brings us closer to who we are born to become.

There are paths we choose
and there are paths that choose us.
What they mean and where they lead —
what keeps us moving forward.

We are not passive recipients of fate.
We are the heroes of our own stories —
shaping each moment,
step by deliberate step.

Whether you face seismic changes
or quiet ripples in daily life,
viewing your path through this framework
recasts everything.
It frames each experience
not as an accident,
but as a stepping stone —
part of the grand, exciting adventure
toward your truest self.

Your trials are neither arbitrary nor aimless.
They aren't obstacles designed to thwart you.
They are catalysts for growth,
a sculptor grinding away at the edges
of your former self,
revealing the person
always waiting within.

Each challenge, each stumble and setback,
is vital work —
the alchemy of transformation.
You are molded
by forces both visible and unseen.
Though the path may be steep —
it is also the fulcrum of your becoming.

This is the gift of the Hero's Journey:
To stride forward with courage,
knowing every trial is not a failure,
but a piece of the larger puzzle of who you are.

It's not only about overcoming —
it's about embracing,
trusting the uncertain road,
finding purpose in the moments
that test you most.

When the way grows dim,
when doubt or frustration
arise to challenge
your commitment to change —
remember:

You are not merely passing through life.
You are becoming.
You are transforming.
You are discovering what it means to live as true you.

Look back at the trails you've walked,
and forward to the paths still ahead.
Know this:
You are the hero.
Your story is still being written,
and with every chapter,
you grow closer
to the self you were always destined to be.

❧

What the Darkness Teaches

The darkest valleys forge the strongest souls,
Where pain becomes the chisel, grief the stone.
What breaks us into pieces makes us whole —
For seeds must split apart before they're grown.

In struggle's grip, beneath the weight of years,
When hope seems just a word for fools to say,
Remember: transformation feeds on tears,
And God's mysterious hand will find a way.

The pain you bear is not without its purpose —
Each wound becomes a doorway to the light.
What seems like endings hidden beneath the surface
Are merely intermissions in your fight.

The tunnel stretches long, the journey hard,
But look: you're still here, breathing, moving forward.
The dimmest flame outlasts the brightest star —
And quiet strength is destiny's true reward.

The brightest promise isn't always dawn —
Sometimes it's knowing you can still go on.
Your greatest joy was born from deepest pain.
The hero rises. And will rise again.

EPILOGUE

"I've led a toothless life. I have never bitten into anything. I was waiting. I was reserving myself for later on. And I have just noticed that my teeth have gone."
— Jean-Paul Sartre

Paralysis by Analysis

We've all been there —
this overwhelming urge to understand everything
before taking action,
to plan every moment,
to seek out every answer.

We tell ourselves we're not ready —
that with more time, more insight,
we'll finally have enough clarity.

Just one more book,
one more expert to consult —
the perfect decision will reveal itself.
And we'll know *exactly* what to do.

But this is how overthinking
disguises itself as wisdom.
This is how preparation becomes avoidance.
How stillness becomes stuckness.
And how clarity becomes a cage.

We get paralyzed by our own thoughts —
trapped in an endless loop of analysis
we can't quite think our way out of.

Perhaps you're doing that right now.
Waiting for the right time.
Waiting to feel ready or a little less afraid.
Waiting for someone to come along
and tell you that today is the day.
The problem with waiting is no one is coming.
The only permission you need is your own.

The antidote to overthinking
isn't more thinking —
it's movement.
Perfect plans don't exist.

The longer we wait for all the conditions
to align just right,
the more time we lose.
The longer we hesitate,
the further away our dreams get.

It's a paradox:
the more we think,
the less we do,
and the less we do,
the further we are from living the life we desire.

Like standing at the edge of a foggy path.
You can see the first few feet clearly,
but beyond that,
everything is blurry, hidden in the mist.

Yet somewhere in that uncertainty
lies the life you're meant to live.

We wait for the fog to lift.
But the path only appears when we begin to walk.
You don't need to see the whole path —
you only need to see enough to take the next step,
and then the next.

Each stride you take pulls the horizon closer.
Each breath, each motion,
teaches you something the mind alone cannot.

What seemed unknowable becomes known —
not through certainty,
but through experience.

We've been conditioned to believe
that perfection is the goal.
We've been taught to wait for the right moment,
the right time, the exact blueprint —
but this isn't how life works.

Life is messy, unpredictable,
and full of twists and turns.
And that's where the magic happens.

Here's the uncomfortable truth:
You don't need a perfect map or all the answers.
You need motion.
You need the courage to take one step,
even if the second one is still hidden.

Because insight without action fades
like morning mist.
But action, even imperfect,
changes everything —
reshaping not just your circumstances,
but your understanding of what's possible.

You've probably felt it:
that urge to get everything right before you begin.

That voice that says,
If I can just figure it all out, I'll finally be free.

But freedom doesn't come from figuring it all out.
It comes from momentum.
From choosing not to wait.
From moving forward without all the answers,
and trusting that the next ones
will meet you on the way.

The people who change their lives
aren't the ones who wait for perfection.
They're the ones who begin.
Boldly.
Imperfectly.
Consistently.

The writer who publishes her first imperfect story
discovers her voice not through endless revision,
but through the feedback of real readers.
The entrepreneur who launches before he's "ready"
learns what customers actually want,
not what he thought they needed.
The person who starts exercising with clumsy form
discovers strength not through perfect technique,
but through the rhythm of showing up daily.

They understand that every great leap
begins with doubt overcome by doing.

Because you can't learn how to swim
by studying the tides.
You have to get wet.
You have to feel the water move around you.
You have to let your body discover
what your mind never could.

And yes — the water will always be moving.
The waves won't wait for your confidence.
But they will teach you how to swim,
how to navigate,
how to keep going.

The real question isn't whether you're prepared.
It's whether you're willing instead —
to let go of the illusion of control,
and trade it for momentum.

You've walked through this book with open eyes
and a receptive heart.
You've traced the arc of transformation,
faced your inner shadows,
discovered your strength,
and learned that courage
is not the absence of fear
but the willingness to begin despite it.

But none of that will transform you
until it moves from thought into action.

So let this be your final reminder:
Everyone's road is different.
You don't need to feel certain.
You don't need to feel fearless.
You just need to begin.

The key to your success lies in taking action —
and not just action, but imperfect action.
That's how you'll learn, grow, and discover
what works for you.

It's through the journey itself that you'll uncover
the lessons you need
to create the life you wish for.
And those lessons, while sometimes hard-earned,
are always worth it.

Clarity lives on the other side of movement.
Your path will not reveal itself before you act —
it will reveal itself because you did.

There's more to explore in the volumes ahead —
layers of the self still waiting to be uncovered.
But don't mistake that for a lack.

You are already *enough*.
You always have been.

So I ask you now:
What one small action have you been avoiding?
What single choice could you make today
that would honor everything you've learned?

So take that first step.
Not when you're ready —
but because you're willing.
Because waiting won't build the life you want.
Walking will.
Starting now.
Starting here.
Starting with this single,
imperfect,
beautiful
step.

∽

ABOUT THE AUTHOR

Andrew Colton is an aerospace engineer and computer scientist by day, and a musician and poet by night — though the lines blur more than he'd care to admit. An award-winning creative and marketing strategist, published author, and educator clutching enough professional certifications to wallpaper a small office, Andrew has somehow convinced some of the world's leading companies — including Cisco, The New York Stock Exchange, IAC/InterActiveCorp, and Neumeyer — to trust him with senior positions.

A serial entrepreneur and professional investor, Andrew has spent countless years navigating the messy, magnificent terrain of transformation — both personal and professional. This book is born from those battles, breakthroughs, and the stubborn belief that growth doesn't require perfection, just honest stumbling in the right direction.

When not writing about the hero's journey, Andrew is likely living one — complete with setbacks, plot twists, and the occasional existential detour. He continues writing, creating, and building — living proof that the quest for meaning requires both relentless ambition and the wisdom not to take yourself too seriously.

This is your invitation to stop merely existing and start truly living — before life leaves you behind.

The Last Method series will continue to explore different dimensions of personal growth and transformation. This first volume lays the foundation: understanding that you are not a passive observer in your life's story, but the hero at its center — and your greatest adventure is just beginning.

For more books and updates:
www.TheLastMethod.com

www.ingramcontent.com/pod-product-compliance
Lightning Source LLC
Chambersburg PA
CBHW050922120626
46552CB00001B/4